Walk Out PROUD

From Hell to Wholeness

A memoir by

Edwin Light

I dedicate this book to anyone
who is hiding his or her sexual
identity. You too can overcome
obstacles and live without fear.
You too can live a joyful and
meaningful life.

Part One

In September '57 I climbed on board the train for Cincinnati and the College-Conservatory of Music. I was 17, fresh out of high school and on the way to my first year in college. Clutching mother's green Samsonite bags, I started walking down the aisle, looking for an open seat. Along the way I noticed a young man in his army dress uniform. When I found a vacant seat, I watched the soldier with his russet brown hair turn round in my direction. I started arranging my gear in the overhead rack and looked a second time. *He's staring at me.* Green as I was, I knew he wanted to be up close and personal. I started squirming, when I felt some stirrings in my crotch.

At the next stop the car cleared, leaving the soldier and me alone. *What to do?* As the sun sank below the horizon, I became more and more excited. *Should I go…? Maybe, he'll…*

While the train car rocked from side to side, over and over again, the soldier turned round and stared at me nonstop. I knew the conductor didn't pass through often…

What if…What if God…? **Two guys?**

I put my longing on hold. I didn't do anything! And the soldier? He stayed in his seat while the train rattled on.

In Kentucky the soldier exited and I went on to Ohio.

That's how I began my college career. Sexually conflicted. I figured, after much frustration, my best option would be…**No** sex. Hey, what's the harm in that?

Even though guys and girls were chasing me, I remained chaste. A miracle, since temptations lurked at every turn.

In junior high, classmates Britt and Johnny invited me to join them for what turned out to be a romp in the pines. The pines, planted by the Civilian Conservation Corps in the 1930s, covered the hill top next to our school. Walking through the grove I could hear and feel the crunch of pine needles under foot and smell the sweet odor of sap oozing out of the trees.

On that summer morning I ogled the boys while they stripped away their clothing, both of them spotlighted by the sun. Their nakedness stunned, thrilled me. Both called to me, "Come on. Have some fun!"

Even though fired up, I said, "I'll just watch." *Should I be **doing** this?*

But what a sight! I had never seen two boys humping. *They're so big, so hard and their pubes… they're shining in the sun!* I watched every move, except for looking round once in a while to see if anyone else was watching.

I grew up in my family's Colonial Hotel in the small Tennessee town of Copperhill, where my classmates had nothing nice to say about queers. "Tommy is a faggot, and he doesn't dare show his face in town." My mother surprised me when she joined the chorus. We were standing in line to pay for lunch at the Read House in Chattanooga when she noticed the cashier. "A pansy!" she said with a sneer. I trembled, as fear walked in.

Yet temptation and desire won out. Weeks later in an outhouse beside Blue Ridge Lake, Johnny of the pine grove and I were pissing and looking each other over. Then he let his trunks slide on down to the floor, showing me more of his blond hair. He started working his big tool; next he reached over and started pulling down on my trunks. "Come on, drop 'em."

"Not many people at the lake today," I noted. Slowly I dropped my trunks, looking at that big dick. Johnny started pressing himself against me and said, "Bend over, you're gonna like it." That's when he cornholed me.

How weird is that! I guess I like being… fucked. When we stepped outside the privy, I waved goodbye to my virginity and wondered, *Will we get together again? Maybe I can…*

Later that day guilt pushed aside all other feelings. By bedtime I was miserable. Mother noticed and sat down beside me, "What's wrong?"

"Today at the lake…Johnny …"

"Yes,… what happened?"

"He pulled down my trunks… It felt wrong. But …."

"What did he do?" she said and pushed back her graying hair.

"He wanted to put his …in my …"

"No!"

"Yes! …And I let him."

"Edwin!"

"I know… I feel so ashamed, but…I was… curious…

"And?"

"And now, now I jus' wanna cry."

A long silence.

"It's alright. It's alright. Don't worry. I'm sure Johnny will join the (Baptist) church soon, and God will forgive him his sin. He'll be redeemed in the Lord." As for me Mother added, "Johnny took advantage of your innocence. That's all. God will forgive you too." That put me at ease, and I fell asleep.

The relief however didn't last long. *I sinned?!*

Even before puberty I had hints, flashes of discovery about who I am. Like the day when Thompson, a tall construction worker who boarded in our hotel, asked me about Tony Fain. Fain, a barber, had just arrived at the Colonial. Thompson, who always spoke plainly and bluntly, had just returned from a new road project in his muddy jeans and boots. We'd had some rain that day. He wanted to know, "Is Fain in drag?" *in drag??* At 12, I had no idea what he was talking about. Thompson saw my puzzled look and added, "Is he a **woman** posing as a **man**?" That question puzzled me as much as the first one. I shrugged. Thompson huffed and walked away.

I'd been weeding our little garden in front of the hotel when Thompson walked by. I finished bagging the weeds I'd pulled and stood up to dust off my knickers, all the while thinking about Fain. *He's young and soft-spoken; he's not like the other men who live here.* Somehow, I felt a connection with the barber. When I walked into the lobby I thought, *Fain won't be welcome in my hometown.*

I knew I was different from the other boys; and I noticed my cousin, Charles Abe, didn't fit in either. His older brothers were forever thorns in my side; they heckled me every time they saw me. Charles Abe, who treated me like a pal, didn't escape his brothers' bullying either.

Charles Abe and I used to play together on the cook's bed in our hotel, while the cook busied herself in the kitchen. Charles Abe, five years older than I, had gone past puberty at the time, while I had another year or two before the 'change.' We tossed and rolled on top of the bed with its box of metal springs jangling. He pulled out my wiener; I put it back in my short pants. We rolled over again, and he popped it out once more. That was the extent of the game as best I can remember. Charles Abe continued to play the game probably because I resisted, sort of. I don't remember touching him. *Was my cousin a homo?* I'm asking myself now.

Charles Abe's father invited me to join him and his three sons for a deer hunt. (I overheard mother arranging this, because she wanted me "to do what men do.") We sat all day waiting for a deer to go by. Not even one passed by. *What a drag hunting is!* They also included me for the tear-down of an old house. (Thanks, mother.) Splinters galore! Charles Abe on both outings stood apart from his kin, who made little effort to draw him or me into their conversations, their laughter. Instead, they hurled digs my way when I said, "Mother told me not to drink any beer today."

"Nana, nana, **Na-Na**, Eddie's tied to her apron strings!" Charles Abe didn't fare any better.

I'd heard through the family grapevine that Charles Abe's daddy beat him. A cousin told me, "I saw Charles Abe running down the road with his dad close behind **waving a belt!**"

In 1952 Charles Abe died in a motorcycle crash near his home. He was only 17. His family assumed he had gone too fast around the sharp curve where neighbors found him. Was he thrilled by speed? Or did he deliberately put himself in harm's way?

Charles Abe lay in a coffin in his family's home/business, that housed on the first floor a restaurant and a large, rental space, with family quarters on the second. Charles Abe's mother, my Aunt Shine, slept on a cot near the coffin, so she could view her son's body whenever she wished, day or night. Her cot and his coffin sat in that empty rental space, stripped of furniture, rugs and curtains, for a week. Her beautiful face, usually radiant, now appeared gray and ever so wrinkled by grief.

Shine often threw her arms over the coffin and cried out, "What should I have done? What could I have done to protect him?" Now I would add, "protect him from his father." Her aching wails filled the blond-brick building. I shuddered. We all shuddered.

I don't remember ever seeing Charles Abe's father anywhere near the coffin.

Because Charles Abe's head was badly damaged on impact with a huge oak tree, it could not be drained completely when embalmed. Regularly, Aunt Shine and others would push back his sandy blond hair and swab blood out of his ears. I couldn't bear to watch. *He's still dying!*

At age 12, when my cousin died, I was troubled by his death, but I didn't fully understand what had happened. Now I'm asking myself, "Did Charles Abe's dad punish him for being gay or for appearing to be gay?" I believe the answer is Yes.

A few months later, after I'd greeted puberty, Aunt Shine opened a magazine to show me a photo. The picture, spread over two facing pages, showed the close-up of a shirtless male weight-lifter from the waist up. Every ripple and nipple were in sharp relief. My eyes probably opened wide; maybe I gasped. I did notice that my aunt watched me intently, while I gazed at the photograph. *Could it be she's looking for signs of queerness?* I'm thinking she was; I'm thinking she wanted to confirm a hunch. I know that I continued to be her favorite nephew.

Charles Abe and I had Shine's love in common.

In September '57 I arrived at Union Station in Cincinnati and made my way by bus to the College-Conservatory of Music campus. I'd had a snapshot view of the campus when I auditioned in May. My attention at that time focused primarily on the audition. Anxiety? Yes, there was some anxiety. After all I was not in my little hometown playing for a church service. Edwin's competing now for admission to a well-known music school.

Eleanor Allen listened to all of us that day. She was so welcoming, she told me, "Come on in," with such a warming smile. Mrs. Allen, a tall, attractive woman full of charm, also distinguished herself as a fine singer, we later learned. All of us auditioning that day agreed, "She's everyone's Mom."

Mrs. Allen made my day, my year with, "Yes, you are accepted for enrollment this Fall." Then she looked over my high school transcript, "Impressive."

In September '57, I entered the freshman dorm where my roommates Gene, a voice major, and Martin, a percussionist, greeted me. Gene, outgoing and gregarious, always wore a big smile; he stood tall and handsome, with brown hair and devil-may-care eyes. Martin, somewhat shy, was always quietly observing; he had auburn hair and lots of freckles. Martin introduced me to the world of percussion ensemble concerts. I heard so many wonderful sounds and compositions I'd never heard.

The freshman dorm for men, formerly a private residence, was a Victorian-era dwelling with a gray stone façade that faced the Conservatory campus on the other side of Highland Avenue. Other Victorian homes filled the campus: Shillito Hall housed C-CM's administrative offices, several teaching studios and a recital space (the former parlor). Shillito had lost some of its original opulence with age; but it did have, with a few cracks, its original stone flooring, checkered in black and white, plus a beautifully carved walnut balustrade leading to the second floor. South Hall, where I had my piano lessons, contained many teaching studios; it too was well appointed. Walking the campus felt very much like a walk in the past with top hat and cane.

The freshman men's dorm stood three stories high with bay windows, a gabled roof and two chimneys on both sides of the house venting fireplaces on the first and second floors. Because of its large bay window, daylight filled our room at the front of the second floor every day.

The double parlor on the first floor served as the gathering space for all the residents. At the beginning of the fall semester our conversations started early in the evening and lasted sometimes till dawn. Topics included our dorm: "Can you believe it? Felice and Scott put Binkley's bed on the roof!"; meals in the school cafeteria; the practice rooms: "Don't sign up for Room 19. You don't want **that** piano!"; the neighborhood; and the faculty.

We often joked about our ear-training instructor Dr. Taylor, a short woman with big boobs, who stood behind a grand piano when she addressed the class. "Her tits will keep her anchored on the Steinway," we all agreed. "She's not going to fall." We were certain her little feet never touched the floor. A theory and composition teacher Dr. Labunski, with his thick foreign accent, pronounced parallel thirds in the music we were studying as 'parallel turds.' We barely concealed our snickering.

At first it seemed college only consisted of partying. "Hey, let's go to Mecklenburg's." Off a group of us would go to the nearby German beer garden for a fun evening. We frittered away another night, and another night. Then exams began. "Are you ready for the sight-singing test?" we dorm-buddies began asking. "What about keyboard harmony?"

Weeks, months had gone by, when reality rudely kicked us in the ass. Oh yes, we're here to be educated, and we're going to be tested. "Geez! We have to study? But we're having so much fun!"

"Somebody got a **D** on the last ear training test?!"
Gotta go.

My roommate Gene introduced me to Dan, a slender and handsome senior, who became Gene's partner in a same-sex thing. I couldn't believe how frank, how brave they were, touching each other. Outside the dorm I felt uncomfortable being with them. They weren't holding hands or anything, but I thought they might.

Dan and Gene studied piano with Herbert Newman who also taught me. Mr. Newman often invited his students to his home that he shared with his longtime partner John Quincy Bass, another piano professor at C-CM, who invited his students as well. Both men were gray-haired; Bass was nearly bald. Newman was the taller and more talkative of the pair. They were probably in their sixties.

Both Bass and Newman were kind and genuinely warm-hearted. "Another night at Bass and Newman's? Can't wait!" All of us piano students would say. We felt so comfortable in their home. In the winter months Bass kept a log fire going that warmed us to the core. "Gene, I need some help over here," Bass called. The two with pokers in hand wrestled some logs that had rolled onto the hearth.

Freshman dorm, C-CM, 1957, Faculty and Staff Welcome, standing l-r, Gene, Herbert Newman, and me; seated, l-r, Scott and Dan, all four were Newman's piano students

Both hosts busied themselves in the kitchen preparing a home-cooked meal eagerly anticipated by homesick freshmen. I'm still making a dessert with green grapes and blueberries I first tasted at their table.

Newman and Bass made no overt effort to persuade me or anyone else to their way of living. They simply demonstrated how pleasant it can be. I heard no talk of homosexuality; I witnessed no groping, no tongues hanging out, because some of the students were straight.

Their longhaired dachshund's tongue did hang out when I visited the Newman-Bass home. The dog was so excited when I walked in, she peed on the spot. After a second puddle, Newman instructed me to, "Call when you leave the dorm, and I will put newspapers on the back porch for her." Problem solved. She emptied her bladder outside and joined me indoors wagging her tail.

Bass and Newman often entertained us with amusing stories. Autumn leaves were tumbling down outside when Newman shared his favorite prank as a teenager back home in Kentucky. "We pushed out-houses over on Halloween night when folks stepped inside." Newman and his cohorts frightened, maybe terrorized their townspeople; but we students were not sitting in those privies, and we howled with laughter.

Looking back, I wonder why the Newman-Bass example didn't inspire me, motivate me. Maybe it did at some level, but I don't remember thinking, *I could have a partnership like that.* As an undergrad I focused on the immediate future: learning a new piano piece, rehearsing with a singer, et cetera. Serious relationships? Not on my mind.

South Hall, C-CM, 1957, Newman's piano studio, 2nd floor front, left side; Bass's piano studio, 2nd floor front, right side. Just a few feet apart.

Newman mentored me not only in music, but also in wine, food, literature, in short, in living the good life. *He's a father to me, the father I never had.*

In my freshman year I felt so unprepared. I'd never had an ear-training class. Yet I had been placed in the most advanced ear training section; and I found it to be a real challenge, earning mostly B's and a few C's, rather than the A's I'd earned in high school.

Keyboard harmony and theory classes were equally daunting, because I'd had no prior experience. History and English comp classes were familiar and much easier for me.

In October I called home for the first time. "You've become a damn Yankee!" Mother spouted after only three words out of my mouth. In a short time, I'd absorbed the sounds around me in Cincinnati. Hey, that's what musicians do. I did mention, "The classes are challenging here. I'm dealing with a lot of new stuff."

In that first semester I struggled to stay afloat in the Conservatory. At Thanksgiving time, I returned to my hometown where I cried in front of my mother and brother.

Sitting in the hotel's parlor, I announced, "I've failed. What am I going to do now?"

"Come on, it can't be that bad. Pull yourself together!"

I didn't want to go back to C-CM; I wanted to stay home.

With my head slung low, I returned to the Conservatory, where, in the second semester, I earned a place on the Dean's List.

———————

I had never before been in a music school surrounded by the sounds of voices and instruments all day every day. I'd had a sampling in high school band and chorus. Our chorus performed twice in the All-State Chorus in the Ryman Auditorium in Nashville with hundreds singing. The musical saturation in a conservatory though leapt beyond anything I'd known. Even though all the activity some days daunted me; I also found it exciting and energizing.

As I passed by the practice rooms, I enjoyed listening to everyone, Felice on trombone, Adrian on oboe, Melissa on piano, working hard to develop their techniques, their sounds, their unique voices. All of that reminded me: *You've got to work, if you want to succeed.* Besides piano lessons I also accompanied the lessons of instrumentalists and vocalists, broadening my knowledge of repertoire and performance.

This is such an inspiring place to be! I've made the right choices: the profession and the school.

After my freshman year at C-CM Britt, a high school classmate, called to say he wanted to come for a visit. Surprised, I paused a moment. "Uhh..., Sure, come on." *Why not?* We knew each other well in junior and senior high. I knew he liked me; and I suspected he wanted to be more than friends.

In May '57 in high school, Britt and I had gone to the Senior Prom together, but not as a couple. Britt and I had never discussed our queerness, had never partnered sexually; even so, we knew we were brothers. We had never talked about making some sort of declaration at the prom. I couldn't; I was clinging to the fence. Britt however smiled broadly as we entered the gymnasium at Copper Basin High.

When Britt visited my efficiency apartment in Cincinnati, we reminisced about home and our classmates. You could easily get cozy in this ridiculously small space. On a regular day, no guests, you could sit on the narrow bed and type away on the manual typewriter situated on a small desk, without moving a leg. Easily, Britt and I reached out and groped each other for the first time. Light-hearted touching for me; it seemed more like a game. (I had of course just stepped over my self-imposed line of no messing around with boys or girls.)

Britt noted my casualness and pulled back. "Are you dating anyone?" he asked.

"I'm dating a girl named Ann, and I'll probably marry her." I hadn't actually thought about marrying Ann, but I liked her a lot, and the feeling was mutual. (I'd just stepped back over my line.)

Britt's smile disappeared. As he stood up, he said under his breath, "I'll see you sometime." He walked out and made no effort to contact me again.

Now I realize how lightly I'd treated an opportunity with a young man who admired me, and who would no doubt succeed professionally. Like his father, the General Manager of the Tennessee Copper Company in our hometown, Britt was pursuing a degree in engineering.

In high school Britt stood out as a tall nerd, who wore bottle-thick glasses. Even though physically awkward he did make the basketball team; he sat on the bench though most of the time. After a year in college, Britt had grown up a lot, gained more poise. *He's more appealing.* But...

I stayed behind my arbitrary line and watched him descend the stairs in my apartment building.

———

At Christmas time that year I hitched a ride home with Alex, a senior voice major. The tenor wowed me with his handsomeness; I sighed, in awe. In the front seat of the car, just the two of us, I could barely breathe. He must have noticed my adoring glances.

Alex graciously dropped me off at the Colonial in Copperhill; and he'd just returned to take me back to Cincinnati. When I started to step inside his black Lincoln town car, Mother grabbed me and kissed me passionately **on the lips!** *Wha... Why?!*

The answer came much later, indirectly so, when Mother told me, "I had to take your father away from two men when I first met him." She offered no details. I assume she meant two pansies claimed my father and they resisted giving him up.

I'm guessing Mother viewed the handsome singer, driving me to Cincinnati, in a similar way that she viewed the two men in 1939. She may have thought, "The tenor is queer (not true) and he's stealing away my son (not true)." *Was she trying to protect me? convert me?*

Mother's kiss remains forever scorched in my memory.

In my sophomore year I pledged the music fraternity, Phi Mu Alpha Sinfonia, encouraged by my piano teacher, Mr. Newman. When the initiation began, bags were given to us pledges to carry everywhere we went. Each bag held a brick and other required items, the biggest being a paddle bearing the fraternity's insignia. We had to collect on the paddle the signatures of all the chapter's members.

If a pledge showed any disrespect for a Sinfonian, which could be the twitch of an eye, he was forced to: "Drink this gallon of water. Hey, you're frowning, drink another gallon!" And, on and on. All this was humiliating and un-professional in my view, and in the eyes of others I later learned.

On the final night of hazing, Sinfonians blindfolded us pledges and drove us to unknown destinations, where we were left to find our way to the next assigned location, and there we would read more instructions. My pledge partner Gary and I were dumped on a country road just outside of Covington, Kentucky. Luckily, we saw a bar down the road, where one of its patrons offered us a ride back to Cincinnati.

"Our destination," we explained, "is Union Station." Our driver however dropped us off just over the Ohio River on a dark street in Cincy. We had no idea where we were and midnight chimes were about to ring. With a few dollars hidden in our clothing, we were able to catch a bus, and then another bus, to the station. We had one close call at a bus stop, when a gang of four young men approached us. Shakily we held on to our paddles till the gang passed us by without even a threatening look. Back at the Conservatory we exhaled, "We made it, without a hitch!"

The highlight of my fraternity experience that year was the national gathering of Sinfonians in Cincinnati. We were so excited to share several days in the company of hundreds of members. We also enjoyed several performances, one of which brought everyone to their feet. When Mary Costa, an opera singer, sang Bernstein's "Glitter and Be Gay" from *Candide*, the whistles and cheers were deafening.

In my senior year I became president of the C-CM Sinfonia chapter. Several of the best musicians in the Conservatory wanted to become members that year, but refused to be hazed. Bill, a gifted composer, spoke for the group, "I'll have nothing to do with that ridiculous initiation." Two or three in this group I assumed were queer.

I discussed the potential members' concern about hazing in a chapter meeting, and we voted to reject it altogether. I spoke with the chapter faculty advisor, Dr. Huston, explaining the reason for the vote. He seemed to be supportive; however, the meeting minutes that included the vote mysteriously disappeared. Soon after I learned the advisor would nullify the vote, if necessary, by contacting his buddies in the national fraternity office.

I was livid when I learned of the advisor's commitment to hazing. The talented musicians who had wanted to pledge refused to join. And, there may have been a bias against homosexuals in the chapter's membership. I had not heard anything specific, but hazing guaranteed their exclusion, at least with the group in queue that year.

The bullheadedness of the advisor and the assumed prejudice of some of the members were in my view limiting the quality of the chapter's membership. I resigned as president and left the fraternity never to return.

The faculty advisor, a formidable opponent, spoke his mind on many issues, and I sat in one of his classes. *How is he going to grade me?* To his credit Dr. Huston separated me from the fraternity and gave me the marks I'd earned. For one of his assignments, I'd arranged a piano piece for concert band. Huston wrote on my manuscript, "Excellent, Ed."

In my junior year I befriended a singer named Scharmal, who had grown up on her family's wheat farm in Kansas. This broad-shouldered, wide-hipped farm girl with brown hair and eyes came into this world with an exceptional soprano voice. I accompanied Scharmal in her voice lessons with Robert Powell, a much-in-demand teacher with many talented students.

Once Scharmal and I visited Powell's house where we saw all of his upholstered furniture covered in thick, clear-plastic wraps. "Does he ever remove the covers?" I whispered. Scharmal and I looked at each other and I mimed, "What kind of nut lives here?" Powell had his quirks, but he was only one of many characters we met at the Conservatory.

Scharmal and I so enjoyed each other's company. She, quick-witted with a language all her own, kept me giddy with laughter. I amused her with stories about my wacky family. Whenever we had a free evening, we often frequented the German restaurant, Mecklinburg's, a few blocks from the Conservatory. Inspired by the balmy summer nights, I said, "Gosh, it's so nice just sitting here under the arbor and the stars." Scharmal nodded in agreement. We were smiling at each other when we clinked our glasses.

The wait staff at Mecklinburg's often took orders brusquely, and they could even be nasty to patrons, especially students. As undergrads we only had a few bucks in our wallets, a fact not lost on the waiters. Scharmal and I, as well as other students, when put off by the staff's imperious conduct, would leave little or no tip. On one of those occasions, our waiter stormed after us through the restaurant and out into the street, shouting, "You ungrateful swine." We chuckled and disappeared into the night.

The two of us continued to socialize until Scharmal completed her undergrad degree. With her Bachelor of Music degree in hand, Scharmal started her college-teaching career in upstate New York. We promised each other we would stay in touch. And we did.

I escorted to the Conservatory's Senior Prom the beautiful, the exotic, Parvin from Persia, whose dark, sultry eyes captivated me. We had shared coffee a few times. On one of those occasions, I had tried to grope her but without success. Parvin wore a girdle that kept her privates out of reach. *I want to know how they feel!*

On the night of the prom, I drank three martinis before leaving my apartment. *Why?* I ask myself now. *Why did I drink so much?*

Drunk, I called on Parvin. I did manage to dance with her without stumbling at the beginning of the evening. As the evening progressed, I walked around our table of eight imbibing everyone's drink. It was more or less a joke: "Look at me. See what I can do!" Someone may have dared me.

Later my head dropped on the table and I fell asleep. When a classmate shook me, I staggered onto my feet, and I knew immediately the liquor I had drunk would soon eject with my dinner and all my abdominal organs. My table mates shouted, "You're an ass." "You're disgusting!" "Get outta here!" All those words bounced off me. I could only hear the rumblings in my gut.

I could see the men's room, but I couldn't walk to it. My legs were locked in some weird gear. I tried to move straight ahead, but I ended up going far to the right. No matter how I positioned my body, no matter how determined I was, I ended up in the wrong place.

I stumbled into the women's room. Passing by the stalls, I waved and spoke to my classmates, "Hi, Sondra. Is this the men's room?" My chatter amused me, certainly not the girls.

After several more attempts I walked into the men's room. The toilet stalls required coins, and I had none. At this point I couldn't contain myself any longer and I threw up in a sink. I filled the sink, I thought, with all I had eaten that day; then I filled another sink.

I felt some relief and a tiny bit sober. I went back to our table, apologized for my behavior and escorted Parvin back to her dorm.

I threw up all night. The next morning, I had to cancel my piano students for the day. I didn't fully recover from my drunken stupor for several more days. That's when I vowed to never repeat that behavior.

Weeks before the prom Parvin had asked me what men do sexually. *Why is she asking me?*

"Do they do it from behind?"

Is she puzzling over who I am?

I mumbled, "On no! I mean, I don't know what men do."

Parvin asked questions, but she had probably already decided, just looking at me: he's a homo and harmless. Prom night she treated me in the friendliest possible manner, tolerating even my drunken stupor.

Soon after the prom Parvin returned to her homeland.

In hindsight, I had probably drunk myself into oblivion to distance myself from Parvin and my true sexual identity.

When I began my graduate studies in 1961 at the Conservatory, I met Gloria, a voice major. As a graduate assistant I became Gloria's instructor in keyboard harmony. Piano playing was not her forte, yet she managed to fulfill the skill requirements. After the class we became friends. Music connected us from the beginning, plus "She sings!" and I enjoyed performing with vocalists. My teacher, Herbert Newman, had told me more than once, "Listen to singers, they will show you how to play a legato line on the piano." I followed his advice.

Gloria invited me to her family's home on the south side of Cincinnati. Her gracious mother welcomed me and introduced me to her husband who had recently suffered a stroke. He could only gesture with his hands since he could no longer speak; and the right side of his body did not flex because of paralysis. Gloria, her mother and her brother, all showed signs of distress and sadness. Gloria's dad, a medical doctor, had had an exceptional career. Now this.

While we sat at the dining table, I saw the family cat pressing on the doctor's paralyzed leg, massaging it. Gloria explained, "We think our cat is trying to revive daddy's leg!"

Weeks later, when my brother came for a visit, I introduced Gloria to Byron. He had just driven up from Atlanta, where he worked as a credit reporter for Dun & Bradstreet. That night he and I for the first time doubledated in his VW Bug. I sat in the back seat with Gloria, he in front with a friend of Gloria's. We dined out, drank some wine and headed back to the Conservatory and the girls' dorm.

At the end of the evening Byron said, "I can't believe how you were mauling Gloria! That was embarrassing!"

"Come on, you've done much more than that!" I replied.

I'd been groping the slender, strawberry-blonde Gloria for sure, but getting nowhere. She too wore a girdle, a chastity belt of sorts that protected her against all intruders. We did kiss, and I did get my hand on one of her tits. I liked the feel of it; and she swooned when I squeezed the nipple.

In the months ahead Gloria completed her undergrad program and pursued her singing career in another state. Years later, we will meet again.

I hadn't been amorously attached so far to a girl or a boy, except for a thing, a fling in high school. Gabe and I had a mini-affair, at least that's what I called it. A private one of course, since Gabe was, for the rest of the world, a hetero.

I idolized Gabe and his athletic build, his muscular arms and thighs. So sexy, so good-looking. Girls swooned when Gabe walked by, and so did I. No doubt he had his share of hetero experiences, but he also spent some personal time with me. **With me!**

At his house when his parents were at work, we stripped and fondled each other. He offered his butt, but we couldn't find a lubricant. Inexperienced me, I couldn't improvise. Maybe he was counting on that. Who cares? I just wanted to be close to him.

Today I view the relationship this way: I was Gabe's boy toy. He could use me anyway he wanted. However, when he said, "Suck me." I stopped short, thinking I shouldn't do that. I singled out fellatio as wrong. *I can't do that. Only queers do that!* I'd drawn a line in the sand of nonsense.

That day or another, we got together several times, I swatted Gabe's crotch (not too heavily); he responded by taking a swing at me as I moved towards the door. "Now you're gonna get it!" he said playfully. He jumped up and chased me into the street, and then block after block in his neighborhood. I ran hard and fast. *He's chasing me!* What a thrill that was!

Our last intimate time took place in the Colonial Hotel, where Gabe joined me for an overnight. I remember the frown on his mother's face when we left his house. Her disapproving look however did not dampen my excitement one bit.

We watched television for a while in the parlor, but my aching heart and body couldn't wait another minute. "Let's go upstairs to Room 19," I said. Mother looked surprised and a little concerned when we left the room. "It's only 8:30!" she said. I didn't care. I'm going to lie next to my idol!

Clothes came off in a flash. We started groping each other as usual; Gabe however couldn't wait a second longer. He mounted me roughly, and soon the semen flew. I don't even remember jerking-off; apparently his orgasm sufficed. As his love-slave I made no demands.

We had no more trysts. Graduation came a few months later and off we went to different colleges. I look back now and sigh. Gabe was my first crush.

After more than five years locked in the closet at the Conservatory, I stepped out of it when I met Tom in the final year of my graduate studies. He was a charmer, a piano major in his senior year, who needed an apartment, and I needed someone to share the rent. We had met several times outside our piano teachers' studios in South Hall, where I told him about my apartment. We talked and looked each other over with more than a little enthusiasm.

Not long after, I showed him around my third-floor walk-up, located directly across the street from the Conservatory in a handsome Victorian house. I chattered away, "It's very convenient, and the rent is reasonable. I know you'll like the landlady; she's especially nice." Tom agreed and signed the lease the same day. With bags and boxes in tow, he moved in the following week.

I initiated the first physical contact (I think I waited until the second night) by crawling into his bed with my face covered in a pale green, smelly cream. That Fall acne had decorated my cheeks and my forehead. *I'm dreaming, no one is going to hug this mug!* Tom however turned out to be tolerant.

I hadn't had sex for a very long time, and Tom? He was as closeted as I. He'd told me about an affair with a faculty pianist that ended abruptly, "He dumped me!"

That night we hesitantly touched each other, while I sniffed the citrous smell of Sauvage Tom had dabbed around his torso. There were some tentative hugs and kisses (*I like the taste of him!*), but no consummations that night. With the church chimes ringing midnight, I looked into Tom's dark eyes while he pushed back his swath of black hair and lit a cigarette. The ashes' glow illumined his face. *He's so good-looking.*

Many passionate nights filled the months ahead. Having squashed my desire in the past, how liberating now to have sex with another man!

When the first-floor apartment became available, Tom and I moved downstairs to a spacious unit that included what had been the parlor and dining room of the house. And we were so happy when we saw the large kitchen and bedroom. "How lucky we are!"

In our new living-room we set up Tom's stereo system. He knew, of course, exactly how to connect all the components. I assisted where needed. When Tom finished assembling everything, I looked around for an on-off switch and clicked on the stereo.

"What?" Tom asked. "You found a switch?!"

"It's right here under the amplifier."

"I didn't know I had a switch; I've been plugging and unplugging the system ever since I bought it!"

I arched my brow.

Christmas was approaching and Tom and I bought a flocked tree we draped with lights that brightened the beautiful parquet floor in the parlor. "'Tis the season to be jolly..."

We were becoming a couple. Tom studied piano with Mr. Bass and I with Mr. Newman. Tom and I, Bass and Newman... We must have thought about, talked about the musical and sexual pairings. We did feel that a halo of sorts had started wrapping itself around us.

We invited classmates over to read aloud Dickens' *Christmas Carol.* Everyone read passages, some taking on specific characters. I was 'Tiny Tim.' We had read most of the *Carol* when our friends began asking,

"Where's the hot cider? the beer? You **promised**!" The evening ended with everyone fully sated and smiling and laughing.

On Christmas Eve I traveled to Detroit to visit my grandparents, while Tom visited his family in northern Ohio.

When we returned to Cincinnati, Tom watched me make my first cherry pie. With no prior experience I made the crust from scratch, rolled it and spread it in the pie tin.

"So far so good. Right, Tom?"

A slight nod.

We had no mixing bowls, so I pulled out the deep Dutch-oven in the top of the stove and filled it with several cans of cherries. "I want this to be so full of fruit!"

"Don't you think that's **too many** cherries?"

I responded with a wave of the hand.

Sugar was added to the tart cherries. Next, I poured the filling into the baked crust and added a trellis top brushed with milk.

Geez, that looks great! I thought.

Tom seemed optimistic.

Out of the oven the pie looked perfect, golden brown with fruit oozing out. The smells of cherries, butter and freshly baked pie crust saturated our whole apartment.

As soon as the pie cooled, Tom and I sat down eager to sample this amazing creation. Tom took the first bite and… grimaced.

"What's wrong?"

"It's so sour!"

I took a bite. "You're right. It's **tart**!"

I checked the Dutch-oven. "Damn, all the sugar's in the bottom!" Looking back at Tom, "I'll try again. I'm sure I'll do better the next time."

But there was no next time. Doubt and fear had been creeping back into my mind steadily over the months Tom and I had been together. Being together with a guy had been my unspoken goal for a long time. I'd hoped it would happen, even though I knew a queer couple would probably not be welcomed by many folks in the U. S. of A. It's not the "land of the free" for everyone.

Fear, fear of being beaten, fear of being maligned, fear of being extinguished, overwhelmed me. I panicked and started packing my bags. When I headed for the front door, Tom appeared; and as I watched his color turn gray, he gasped and said, "I don't understand. Why? We've been getting on so well. How am I going to explain this?... I **trusted** you."

"Tom, it's not you. I can't handle it. I can't be queer."

A faculty pianist had abandoned Tom, and now I'd turned my back on him. He didn't deserve it. Tom was a kind and generous person. Now **he** had to answer our classmates, "Why did Edwin move out? What's going on?" Some would assume he caused the break-up.

A few blocks from the Conservatory I rented a room. *I'll feel much better here, separated from Tom.* Instead, I felt so alone and lost. I dragged myself to classes and the practice rooms. I escaped my misery only a few hours a week, when I went to the suburbs for my organist/choir director job.

Close friends did ask, "What's up?"

"Oh, I just need to have my own space," I replied, grinding my teeth. *What the hell have I done?*

Up to that point everything had been going smoothly. I'd been practicing my graduate recital and wrapping up the one remaining course for the master's degree. Now the ground had fallen out from under me. Or, to be precise, **I** had **knocked** the ground out from under me.

I chatted with a fellow grad student, Suzanne, in my new room. "I feel miserable. I don't know what to do? What do you think I should I do?"

"First of all, slow down! Relax."

We sat in silence for a while.

Suzanne lay back on my bed, offering a solution to my dilemma. Not a word was spoken.

*I'm **not** going to climb on top of her.*

Eventually she sat up, and we walked silently back to the Conservatory.

Soon after I left Tom, I went to the Dean at C-CM and told her, "I no longer want to study piano with Herbert Newman."

With Newman's guidance I had completed my undergraduate degree, and now I approached the completion of my master's. Newman stood tall as an unapologetic, self-assured homosexual, who welcomed me for five-plus years in his studio, and in his home where he lived happily with his partner John Quincy Bass. Neither Bass nor Newman had tried overtly to convert me; they had simply shown me their successful union.

When the Dean informed Mr. Newman of my decision, Newman immediately called me to his studio. I could barely lift my feet up the steps in South Hall, where he waited for me on the second floor. Newman had supported me in all my studies, he had befriended and trusted me. And, he had been a father to me.

"I'm leaving Newman's studio because of his sexuality," I'd told the Dean.

When I entered his studio Mr. Newman said, "You've treated me like a dog! How can you do this after all these years?" I tried to answer, but I couldn't utter a single word. I turned round and walked out in tears, realizing how brutally I'd severed our relationship.

Two weeks later Mr. Newman knocked on the door of my new home. Shocked and apprehensive, I stepped back when I saw him. He spoke a few words, stepped forward and… **groped** me! I recoiled and pushed him back, quickly closing the door behind him. Newman had never touched me that way. Maybe, he thought he could resolve my ambivalence. "**Groping** me?! That's **not** the thing to do," I said out loud.

Trembling, I sat down and felt oh, so alone. I stared for the rest of the afternoon at the blank walls in my little room, my cell, my hell.

I had started the master's degree recital program with Herbert Newman. In the remaining months of 1963, I continued the preparation with Miriam Kockritz, who had been my accompanying teacher. She ranked high as a musician by me and many others.

Practicing the recital repertoire Newman had chosen for me, reminded me of our estrangement and the harm I had done, leading to more emotional distress.

I didn't want to perform the recital. Under duress I played the required jury in front of the piano faculty with Newman and Bass present. Neither uttered a word or looked at me.

Because I had a good reputation many attended my recital. I looked into the audience and recognized friends and faculty who had come to support me. But my longtime mentor and ally Mr. Newman did not attend, nor did his partner, nor did Tom.

I felt so alone on that stage.

When I started playing Beethoven's *Sonata, Op. 110*, I couldn't feel the keys. Numbed by my usual performance anxiety, but more powerfully, numbed by the feeling of denial and alienation.

Damn! I keep repeating the opening of the Scherzo. **Move on!**

I desperately wanted to run away. This must be hell, the one preachers rail about.

The rest of the program, including Chopin's *Sonata in B Minor*, sounded more like echoes. *How soon can I leave the stage?* The more I played, the more I panicked. *Hurry up, clock!*

I made some missteps in the Chopin. *I know the Finale, damn it! Where am I? Which key?* I faltered, but I got back on the horse for the gallop to the finish line.

Afterwards when I would normally have greeted the audience, I disappeared into a studio, leaving behind me a long line of friendly faces. One of my classmates Melissa, another pianist, found me and said, "You played well!" I assessed it differently: the recital was a failure. *I'm a failure.*

The next day in analysis class Dr. Taylor said, "We waited a long time in the reception line to speak with you." I mumbled and looked away.

The performance was probably better than I remember, but I felt unhinged throughout the evening. That sense of failure on stage, forged by my sexual denial, became a major turning point in my life and career that haunted me for years to come.

Part Two

With my master's degree completed at C-CM and no jobs in sight, I moved back to my hometown in 1964. Before I could apply for another job, I had to acknowledge an obligation, military service.

"If you want to avoid the draft and a tour of duty in Vietnam, join the Army Reserves," a friend had told me. I soon volunteered for the Reserves, a commitment that required one weekend of training each month for six years, plus two weeks each summer. That all seemed overwhelming at first, until the years started going by more quickly than I imagined. Most importantly, all those years were **stateside.**

And now, basic training. After six years in a Conservatory, one might say, sheltered in a Conservatory, this 24-year-old entered boot camp. Nothing could have been in sharper contrast.

When I arrived at Fort Jackson, South Carolina, Uncle Sam immediately transferred me and many other recruits to a holding camp called Leesburg, because a backlog of trainees had already filled the Fort's barracks. At Leesburg we warmed ourselves with pot-bellied stoves (it was winter), and we relieved ourselves in out-houses. We all adjusted quickly more or less, and we appreciated life back home even more.

In Leesburg I soon lost count of the weeks we were there. The days, the weeks became a blur of calisthenics. The exercises were interrupted only occasionally by 'duck-walking:' we picked up cigarette butts while strolling in a squat. The instructors had little else for us to do since the official training would not begin until we returned to Fort Jackson.

Sometimes the instructors pressed too hard with the exercises. One recruit was singled out for some ridiculous reason. "Okay, Stanley, drop and do 50 push-ups! Now 50 more! Now..." Stanley collapsed and lay motionless on the ground. An ambulance had to carry him away, and he never returned.

I discovered an alternative to the endless exercising: kitchen police. I volunteered for kitchen duty often. In the mess hall the head honcho barked our orders for the morning, "Hey, Henshaw, dump all these bags of potatoes in the peeler. Jones, you slice the carrots and onions. Light, Crawford, Billings, Parker, over here. Mix this burger meat with some salt and pepper." We mixed the ground beef and the seasonings with our hands, no gloves required. Some of us scratched ourselves or wiped our noses from time to time, then back we went to the beef in the giant-size bowl.

At last, we moved back to Fort Jackson, where I met my training company that consisted mostly of troops just out of high school. At 24, I was the 'old man' of the outfit.

I laughed when the medics inoculated our company. Full of bravado, the jocks bragged, "That's chicken shit. We can do that. It's **easy!**" I couldn't stop chuckling when they cringed in the vax line. More than a few jerked away as the injection guns touched their shoulders. A lot of "Damns!" and a few "Shits!" filled the room. The powerful vaccine streams had gashed their upper arms. The wounded boys limped away.

Probably no photos exist of the anal probe of recruits, but what a sight it was to look round as dozens of bare bottoms were turned towards the center of the room. The medical team stood poised behind those butts with gloved and greased fingers. In my fantasy, "Hey Docs, take a break. I'll do the probing with my dipstick."

The younger recruits eagerly anticipated another day on the rifle range, all wanting to aim right and qualify for the highest rating. I loathed firing the M14 rifle day after day. Because of the noise, I held the rifle as far away from my head as possible. Still, the gunfire jarred my right ear. Later an audiologist told me the opposite ear suffers the hearing loss. And that's true in my case.

I'd had no prior experience with guns. I would have preferred using rocks and a slingshot. Somehow, despite all my efforts to the contrary, I qualified as an Expert Marksman, much to the chagrin of my younger cohorts who did not qualify.

The noise of the rifle was not music to my ears, nor was the music I heard in the barracks from the recruits' radios. After six years in the Conservatory, where classical melodies wrapped my world, I was dulled, numbed by all the recorded sounds around me: country-western, rock and roll, and pop. I often reminded myself, *Boot camp won't last forever. The time is coming when I'll go back to the musical world I miss so much.*

Week after week at Fort Jackson I felt much frustration as a closeted, 24-year-old gay. Every day I looked at many young men in their physical prime: showering, shaving, pissing in the troughs, sweating through their uniforms and forever flexing their muscles. And no gay dudes in sight. That was more visual stimulation than I could bear; and we rarely had a minute alone. One day at the rifle range I had one of those minutes. I walked into a cluster of shrubs and jerked off. *Oh, my god!* I couldn't believe the powerful, high-arcing stream that flew out of me.

Our drill sergeants pressed us hard every day to ensure we were ready for whatever was out there in the trenches. We understood, but I resented their demands delivered with threats and curses like, "You yellow-bellied cock-suckers." Late one night I spotted a drill sergeant's motorboat parked outside my barracks. This sergeant wasn't the toughest of the bunch, but he was one of **them**. I pissed on his boat from one end to the other, venting my repressed desire for revenge. Bladder emptied, I sighed. *How **sweet** is this!*

Our company, maybe all companies, had a Beetle Bailey. Like the comic-strip character, our goofus often entertained and sometimes rattled us. Bill, our Beetle, qualified for a truck-driver's license much to everyone's surprise. On his first trip out, he parked his truck, completed an assignment and then returned to where he thought he had left the truck. "I couldn't find it," he told us, after he walked back to Fort Jackson.

Days later we were tossing live grenades out of concrete, U-shaped bays. The instructor explained how to pull out the pin and throw the explosive. When I released the pin, all I could think was, *Hurl this damn thing as far as possible.*

"That's one helluva throw!" the instructor said, nodding his head.

Lucky me, Bill the Beetle waited his turn in the bay next to mine. Rather than lob the grenade over the wall in front of him into the impact area, he threw it over the dividing wall between us. "Hit the dirt!" the instructor yelled. We all dropped face-down, hands over heads. The grenade bounced off the front wall of my bay and exploded where it would do no harm. *Whose side are you on, Bill?*

Near the end of basic training, we crawled under barbed-wire with rifles in hand. Live rounds of machine-gun fire passed inches above our heads. To remind us of the potential danger (if hearing the rounds wasn't enough), tracer bullets flew over us at regular intervals. We **hugged** that ground and watched those tracers fly over our heads. *This is beginning to feel like the real thing.*

I made it through basic, and I made it through the years and commitments required by the Army Reserves. I also learned several life lessons: Be prepared, stay fit and stay alert.

After boot camp I returned to my hometown, where First Methodist hired me to direct the choir. And, in the weeks ahead I began teaching piano to several children.

This is not my goal! I want to teach piano at the college level. I adapted nonetheless. I had to.

<hr>

In Cincinnati I had visited several churches, Episcopal, Catholic, Unitarian-Universalist, in my quest for a spiritual home. For a time, I considered other options, such as agnosticism, atheism and humanism.

I'd been reared in the Southern Baptist Church, where mother began taking me to services when I was a child; and, a few years later, she began nudging me to follow in her footsteps to the altar. Soon the Baptist preacher added his voice. He pressed me to be baptized, cleansed of the sins with which I was born, and to "seek salvation in the Lord Jesus Christ, ensuring your entry into heaven."

Literal interpretation of the Bible had been the norm in the Baptist church from its beginning. Any doubts, any questions about the Book were rarely asked since the Bible held the ultimate truth. Prodded by my Sunday School teachers I memorized some of the Psalms, the Beatitudes and other passages from the Holy Book. The minister urged us young people to memorize the names of all the books in the Bible.

The 'fire and damnation' sermons each week were directed at those of us bound for hell. I resented being pressured by the minister and by my mother. I had questions. *Why do I need to walk to the altar for forgiveness?* My unholy reaction: do that very walk just to get people off my back. I'd just turned twelve.

As I approached the baptismal pool, I recalled two near-drowning experiences, one at age six walking into the surf in Southern California and one near home in Lake Lamar when I was eleven. Full immersion frightened me, but there was more: "**Why** are we doing this?" I asked a classmate behind me. Tommy had no doubts; he became a Baptist preacher.

I of course survived the immersion. In the years that followed I behaved like a good Baptist, doing what the preacher expected of me. I sensed though that wasn't the end of it.

———

When I returned home from Ft. Jackson, I decided to be honest with the minister at First Baptist. I told him to remove my name from the church's rolls. The minister instantly responded, "If you try to persuade anyone to your point of view, I will stop you in your tracks!" He surprised me with his anger, his arrogance and his inflexibility. *What does he imagine my 'point of view' to be?* I'd not said a word about it.

That same day the minister informed my mother of the decision. Damn! I wanted to tell her myself. She came home from work that afternoon crying nonstop. "Where did I fail you?" she asked.

No matter what I said, she cried.

Later that night mother and I were watching television. She dozed a while, then half awake, she stood up and turned off the TV in the middle of the program I was watching. "God dammit! Mother, turn it back on!"

With total conviction she responded, "Tomorrow you will sit with me in church. If not, don't be here when I get back!"

I didn't go to First Baptist, nor did I pack my bags. I waited for her. She walked in, but she wouldn't look at me.

"You're still here," she said.

"Don't you think it's **un-Christian** of you to treat me this way?"

She sobbed for the rest of that day and the next. Quietly over several more days, with few words spoken, we came to an uneasy truce. Mother in time stopped trying to save my soul; and I continued my search for a spiritual harbor.

Later I learned the Southern Baptist Convention condemned homosexuality, calling it an abomination; and it still does today.

Mother continued to introduce me to single women in Copperhill. "You'll really like Sally!"

I went out with two school teachers briefly. They were attractive and interesting, but...

The stress of hiding my sexuality wore me down. I couldn't confide in anyone. The negative attitude toward queers in my hometown had not changed since my high school days. In boot camp the drill sergeants' pet phrase to motivate us, "Shape up, you yellow-bellied cock-suckers!", served only to alienate me. The frustration spilled over...

During this time I became my most severe critic about everything I did, said or thought. Confidence began evaporating. I could still hear Mother's voice, "Hey, stupid!", whenever I fumbled a task in grammar school. When I left the Conservatory, I had doubts about my musical ability; and now I wondered if I would ever have a job in academia. That's when I started stomping, stomping on every little thing I considered to be flawed in my day-to-day behavior. **Every little thing.**

A year later I reconnected with Gloria, my friend from Cincinnati days. She told me about a piano position at the school where she taught singing. I applied and Clifford Julstrom, department chair, offered me a piano position on the music faculty at Western Illinois University. *This is what I've been hoping for!*

When I arrived in Macomb, Illinois, Gloria greeted me with open arms, "Welcome to Western! I'll walk you around campus, and introduce you to the faculty."

Gloria and I renewed our friendship over cups of coffee around town and over home-cooked meals in her apartment. She brought me up to date on her family; and we recalled our years at the Cincinnati Conservatory. I walked away thinking, *Could* **we** *be more than friends?*

One night in her apartment Gloria and I stripped and fornicated for the first time. And, it was my first time in the sack with a female, and I enjoyed it. In the months ahead we did it again. *I love the feel of me inside her.* One night I mounted her repeatedly, while she lay there indulging me. *What's the tally? Six?*

"Gloria, how was it for you?" That's the question I rarely asked. Later I heard Gloria's complaint through the grapevine, "Edwin only fucks, when **he** wants to!"

I also became aware there were opportunities to connect with the queer brotherhood at Western. I only needed to knock on the studio door next to mine to meet Burt, the tuba instructor.

The relationship that developed with Burt was complicated. *He's married with children.* And I couldn't make up my mind about him or about me. Should I or shouldn't I get involved?

Burt resolved my indecision by knocking on my apartment door. "Is this a good time?" he asked. Startled, I hesitated, then said, "Come on in," while I looked over his shoulder to see if his wife had followed him.

"Nice apartment," he said, looking around my new home. "It's roomy," I replied. All the while, we're looking hungrily at each other. Burt stepped forward and embraced me, and I swooned. I tried to unbutton and loosen his clothing, but my nervousness got in the way. With ease Burt removed my shirt and pants. My hands fumbled when I touched his body, while his hands, and then his tongue, set me on fire. I gasped when he swallowed me whole. My body began to jerk; I reeled. I was howling like a coyote, when the bed collapsed to the floor.

"That's ha-larious!" Burt shouted. We both laughed loud and long. Much of my anxiety evaporated on the spot. In the months ahead Burt and I shared more time together. During those months he moved to a house of his own, when he and his wife decided to terminate their marriage. *A future with Burt?*

A future with Gloria? A future with Burt? I continued to straddle the fence. And those pickets were becoming more and more uncomfortable.

In the fall of '67 I played my first solo recital at Western. *How's this going to go?* I managed somehow to pull together enough confidence to play well and be applauded by faculty and students. However, to reduce my time on stage, I'd eliminated the repeated passages in Schumann's *Symphonic Etudes.* "Please play all the repeats, so we can fully savor the composer's creation," a colleague told me after the concert.

In the next several years I soloed with the University Orchestra three times. First time out I played Franck's *Symphonic Variations.* I so enjoyed the piece, my first ever with orchestra. The *Variations* inspired me with their full-blown romanticism.

Next, the orchestra conductor invited me to play Rachmaninoff's *Second Concerto.* During the time I learned the music, I became anxious. *What have I taken on? Do I need more facility? More solo experience?* Confidence began to wane. In hindsight I probably should have worked the concerto with a coach.

At the performance I felt inhibited in front of the audience, in contrast with rehearsals where I was outgoing and expressive. "That's beautiful!" Rebecca told me. She played on another piano the orchestra part for rehearsals. In a rehearsal with orchestra one of the woodwind players said for all to hear, "I didn't know the piano could sing!"

"Good show!" Rebecca told me in the reception line after the public performance. I interpreted her remark as being less than high praise.

I did play a third time with the orchestra, Stravinsky's *Movements for Piano and Orchestra.* I played this piece very well. Still, the uncertainty I felt with Rach II, led to much reflection.

Looking back, I should have solved the problem, gained the confidence, instead I chose to run away from it.

Should I be playing solo repertoire? On really bad days, *Should I stop playing the piano altogether?* My grad recital in Cincinnati still cast its shadow.

A few months went by. "Accompanying singers, that's what I do best," I told Rebecca. I had given up being a soloist.

The following year I founded at Western the *Song Recital Series* that featured faculty singers and pianists. I arranged the programming and performed in all the *Series* concerts, which became an annual part of Western's music programming

Scharmal, my friend from Cincinnati days, and I decided in July of '69 to attend the Aspen Music Festival in Colorado with funding from teaching fellowships. Scharmal and I had kept in touch with letters and an occasional phone call.

Early on we went horse-back riding in the Rockies. The mountain scenery was as beautiful as the music we heard at the Festival, Juilliard's best. And, what a delight to get away from my worrisome concerns at Western.

One afternoon a group of us lunched lakeside with the Dells towering above. When we spotted a waterfall above us, I said, "Hey, let's climb up! It can't be too far away." Six of us agreed to start the climb. Scharmal stayed behind. "Too much climbing for me," she said.

The higher we went, the more challenging the climb; and the higher we went, the cooler the temp. We were wearing sandals and shorts.

After an hour four people dropped out saying, "It's too risky!" A fourteen-year-old boy named Bobby, the 1969 National Baton-Twirling Champion, and I pushed on. Looking the twirler over, *He's a cute kid, probably a gay one.*

The climb became treacherous. After a while we could only find toe-holes and finger-holes in the rock face. We shimmied around massive rock formations searching for an easier way up. Going down, a sheer drop-off, looked impossible. *There must be a way out of this!*

When we came to a halt, Bobby started crying. I reviewed the possible places to ascend. "I'll climb up here over this out-cropping, and I'll give you a hand," I told him. The tearful baton-twirler was too afraid to move. "Maybe someone will rescue us," Bobby said as he leaned back in a granite niche. I wanted to console him, hold him; but survival topped all priorities that afternoon.

I began to push up with my toes and pull up with my fingers, inching up slowly. I tried again and inched up a little more. It became clear if I wanted to go any farther, I would have to rely exclusively on my fingers and hands. *I'll have to release my toe-hold.* This became the moment of truth. *Will I be brave and press on?*

I pulled up with all my strength and released my feet. Next, I saw a lush green meadow skirting the mountain. *Have I died and gone to heaven?*

I sat there for a couple of minutes looking around and shaking my head. *Am I seeing clearly?* I leaned forward and touched the grass. *It's real!*

I called down to my fellow climber, "I made it! You can do it too." He slowly took my hand. As soon as he was up, we followed the grassy ridge around to a shale slide that looked harmless. We were able to walk over it without a hitch, though some pieces did skitter down the mountain side.

The sun was now touching the horizon. Bobby and I hurried along and looked for a trail but found none. We were making our way, we hoped, back to lakeside and our friends.

"I hope they're still there," I said.

"Me too," Bobby added.

Finally, we stepped off the mountain not far from the lake.

"We're back on level ground!" I said with all the volume I could muster.

"At last!" Bobby said with tears still rolling down his cheeks.

Our voices were echoing around us when a park ranger approached, "Are you Edwin? Bobby?" We nodded. "Your friends told me you went up the mountain hours ago. I just alerted a search party."

The three of us were walking toward the parking lot, when the ranger added, "You guys are lucky! We lose one or two climbers every year on that slope."

We could have died up there, I thought. Bobby went ashen.

Our friends arrived soon after and gave us the hugs we sorely needed.

That day we never saw the waterfall, never felt its spray. Bobby went his way, I went mine.

A few days later I felt the full weight of what had happened. *One or two climbers a year?* "Damn, am I lucky!"

"You have a guardian angel protecting you," a palm-reader had told me several years before.

I'd entered the palm-reader's little room wondering, *What will I learn, if anything?* When she took my hand and scanned the palm, she said my mother had suffered a fall in her youth. *That's true! How does this stranger know that?* She mentioned more events in my past, also true. "Look," she said, "Here's your lifeline, and here's a line running beside it. You have a guardian angel protecting you." *I have a guardian angel.*

At the Aspen Festival the Juilliard String Quartet held open rehearsals of the late Beethoven quartets with comments that totally captivated Scharmal and me. What extraordinary musical knowledge and insights! Shirley Verrett sang a recital of art songs and arias from *Carmen* that dazzled everyone. The days and nights were filled with wonderful music-making. We returned to our university teaching posts overflowing with inspiration, Scharmal to East Texas State, me to Western Illinois.

Scharmal and I had bonded again. We were such good friends. Our paths had crossed in Cincinnati and now Aspen. Cincinnati, we had chosen independently; Aspen, we had selected together.

Scharmal waved wistfully as she drove away.

I felt a powerful attraction to men, more so than my attraction to women. Sex with Gloria I enjoyed, and folks approved. Closeted me couldn't be happy though being a homo. After a sexual high in bed with Burt, I felt like I had committed a crime. I asked myself, "How can I escape this prison, my mind?"

Uncertain on stage and ambivalent in the bedroom, I sought counseling with Dr. Campion, a psychiatrist.

"I'm here because I can't live with my attraction to men, can't shake off the stigma. I want to go straight."

The doctor reflected for a minute or two. He broke the silence with, "You've made a wise choice, and I can help you. Are you ready to begin?"

The first months were especially painful with the probing of my psyche, bringing back disturbing memories, like my father's indifference that cut me like a knife. *Is therapy worth all this distress, and all the expense?* At the time I thought I had no other option.

I met with Dr. Campion every week, sometimes twice a week in the beginning, for what became a four-year period. More than once I told him about my experiences with my colleague Gloria. He always asked, "What about the foreplay? The penetration? Did she have an orgasm? Did you? How satisfying was it for you? For her?" The doctor salivated when I shared the details.

Campion cheered me on. I pursued women, both faculty and students, with enthusiasm and curiosity. This for me was a grand adventure, besides being a path to redemption.

One unexpected opportunity came my way. A faculty wife whom I barely knew stalked me in the university library and later in town. "My husband is impotent. He has a rare and incurable disease," she explained. "I want you to be my lover." Her boldness stunned me. I shook my head and walked away.

I did not encourage her, yet she persisted. When I was shopping one day in the supermarket, she showed up with one of her young children. *You brought your daughter?!* I was really uncomfortable. *Are you crazy?* After another refusal she gave up her campaign.

For my first-ever trip outside the States I flew to Paris in August, 1970. I needed a break from teaching and my concerns at home. I was thirty and eager for an adventure, even though anxiety reminded me: *I'll be traveling solo to a foreign country and speaking, or trying to speak, another language.* I jittered as I climbed on board the plane.

I chose France because I'd studied French in college with considerable interest, and I knew about my French ancestry through a cousin, Max Gartrell. Max had researched my grandmother's family history back to the 17th century when our Huguenot ancestors had fled Catholic persecution. Some had landed in Virginia and made their way over time to north Georgia where my grandmother was born in Whitestone in 1881. Her homestead has been the gathering place for Gartrell reunions for many years.

The Cincinnati Conservatory had introduced me to French piano music, and I enjoyed then and now listening to and playing the music of Ravel, Debussy and Poulenc. Ravel's *Jeux d'eau* lifts my spirits whenever I play it.

Luckily, before I left the States, I met a visitor from Paris enrolled in the École Polytechnique, preparing for a career in civil service. Myriem Mazodier was probably in her late-twenties with darting dark eyes behind her black-rimmed glasses. She invited me to visit her family near the Bois de Boulogne. *I'll know someone in Paris!*

I landed at Orly Airport, shuttled into the city and hailed a taxi. On the ride to the travel agency with nose pressed against the window, I saw the Eiffel Tower, Notre Dame and so much more! Blissful, I entered the travel office and showed an agent my list of all the things I wanted to do. "You can't possibly do all this in ten days!" he explained. Deflated, I asked, "What is possible?" When he told me what I could do, my spirits climbed back to blissful.

The same day I phoned Myriem, who told me to, "Join us tomorrow evening for dinner. Please come at eight." She gave me the address and directions by bus. Along the way I noticed several Parisians were not friendly. The bus driver, for one, begrudgingly answered my queries. Other American tourists had told me to expect unfriendliness, even rudeness.

At her family's apartment Myriem introduced me to her mother, brother and uncle who spoke much of the time to me in English. "I didn't know my uncle spoke English so well," she told me in the kitchen. I welcomed a familiar tongue, since speaking in French became exhausting, especially so since the meal stretched from eight o'clock to midnight. Soup, entree, salad, dessert ... brandy. The uncle introduced me to his favorite, "You must try Armagnac." I did, and I liked it.

As we said our goodbyes, Myriem invited me to meet some of her friends at their apartment near the Palais de Justice the following evening. When I arrived for the dinner party, Myriem greeted me at the door and walked me through the spacious apartment handsomely furnished with what appeared to be antiques. *A few coins here.*

Myriem introduced me to Robert, a fellow poli-sci student, who, as the eldest son of his family, hosted the party. The parents were spending the month of August in the French countryside to escape the heat and the crush of tourists. Robert, like Myriem, was in his late twenties. He briefly looked me over and walked away, while Myriem introduced me to Robert's sister and her fiancé, the heir to Napoleon Brandy, and to Robert's brother. All three were in their early twenties and nattily dressed.

At the dinner table no one spoke English, save for Myriem who offered me an occasional word or two. I only heard rapid-fire French that left me in the dust. I didn't feel welcome. Robert, the host, was especially aloof.

After the meal we moved to couches and comfy chairs in the large dining room. I sighed with relief, when the young bridal couple asked me in English about my travel plans. I walked them through the list of towns I would be visiting with Avignon as the first stop. While they shared some of their adventures in the south of France, a story came to mind.

"Where will you be going for your honeymoon?" I asked.

"Like all our friends we go to the Greek Islands."

"Will you have a chaperone while you're there?"

The couple laughed. "You making the joke. Yes?" The others in the room were beginning to show some interest in what I was saying.

"My Great Aunt Fanny dominated her daughter's life," I continued. "When her daughter married, Aunt Fanny insisted on accompanying the couple on their honeymoon." I now had the attention of everyone in the room, including the arrogant host.

"Not only did she travel with them, she slept between them on their wedding night!"

"No!"

"That can't be true?!"

"*Incroyable!*"

"But it **is** true," I proudly said, knowing I had shattered the ice that had surrounded me at the dining table. All were laughing and smiling at me.

The French do enjoy a good story.

Wine flowed again, while Myriem told everyone, "Edwin plays the piano." We moved into another room where the group asked me to play the upright piano. I played one score after another: a Beethoven sonata, a Debussy prelude, whatever someone put in front of me. At the end of the evening Robert invited me back for a tour of Montmartre the following night. *I'm in!*

On the way out Myriem explained, "Robert hates Americans. Now he's changing his attitude, at least for you."

I'm glad I visited Robert and his siblings. I gained so much by engaging with the 'enemy,' breaking down walls and connecting with another culture. Otherwise, I would have just been passing through France.

Before I set out on my trip to France, I'd heard the label "ugly American," and in a Paris train station I observed two college-age boys who qualified. The pair entered the cafe in Gare St. Lazare and started looking at *le menu.*

'What's this? I can't read this," one of them said. The other tossed his menu on the table. When the waiter asked in French what they wanted, the two looked at each other, one miming "What's with this guy?" And, they proceeded to order in English. The waiter shrugged. The Americans decided to speak louder; the waiter shrugged again, hands in the air. They spoke even louder; then tension and silence filled the space.

I walked over to rescue the waiter, who'd turned crimson. "Why doesn't he speak English?" asked one of the pissed-off boys.

"This is not America. You're in **his** country." Seeing the lack of charity in their faces, I switched to, "What do you want to eat?" They gave me their order which included boiled eggs. *Boiled eggs?* I didn't know the idiom for boiled eggs, so I explained as best I could by putting an egg in hot water... That was enough for the waiter who left to place the order. The boys thanked me, and so did the waiter.

Later the same day I trained to Avignon for my next adventure in Provence. In the dining car when I scooped out a melon with a spoon, I became aware a French family was watching me. When I looked round at their table, I saw the parents and two children slicing their melons with a fork and knife ever so precisely. The parents' faces clearly expressed displeasure at my 'barbaric' method.

On my first full day in Avignon, I began to explore the city. First stop, a sidewalk cafe for breakfast, where the waiter brought me a large cup of steaming coffee, a plate with plump croissants hot out of the oven, a bowl of creamery butter and a bowl of orange marmalade that sparkled in the morning sun. *This must be heaven!*

Every day in Provence produced a new revelation. When I visited the Palais des Papes in Avignon, a Picasso exhibit of erotic paintings startled me, not by their frankness, but by their appearance in the Popes' Palace. Then I learned some of the Popes hadn't deprived themselves of sensual pleasures. When I stepped off the train in Aix-en-Provence and started walking down the Cours Mirabeau, I jerked to a halt. *I've been here before!* That feeling of *deja vu* convinced me: I have a French connection!

The adventures, I'm happy to say, did not end on my last day in France. When I checked in at Orly, I heard, "There are no coach seats left."

"What? I'm supposed to leave today. What am I going to do?"

"We do have a seat for you in First Class…at no extra charge."

Did I get that right? First class at no extra charge?!

Even when seated, I still couldn't believe it. My long legs could move without cramping. I wasn't shoulder to shoulder with the next passenger. *Air France, I won't forget!*

Soon we were airborne and the champagne began to flow. A steward handed me a dinner menu. *These choices are amazing.*

The steward said, "We recommend hearts of palm, pigeon breast..." I'd never had either one. "I'll have both."

The passenger in the seat next to me suggested with his French accent, "You should order the duck in orange sauce for your entree. It's prepared on the plane."

So began our conversation as we flew over the Atlantic. I explained I'd been traveling for the first time to France, and I spoke about my days in Provence.

My fellow traveler pulled out a portfolio of watercolors he had just painted. "I grew up in Provence. I come back every summer for six weeks." He showed me beautiful paintings of places I had visited. With every page-turn, tears streaked his cheeks. His love for Provence, for France, moistened my eyes too. *What luck! I've had a memorable holiday in France, and now I'm traveling first class with this extraordinary passenger.*

When we exchanged names, my fellow passenger told me without fanfare, "I'm Charles Masson; I live in New York City. I own the restaurant *La Grenouille.*" At the time I didn't know the restaurant's reputation. Later, I learned 'The Frog' ranked as one of the best French restaurants in New York.

Monsieur Masson and I continued to share stories about Provence, while we drank more sparkling wine. Hours passed and I began dozing off with sweet dreams of my days in *la belle France.*

After a wonderful sojourn in France, I resumed my sessions with a psychiatrist, who encouraged me to visit with my friend Scharmal. Dr. Campion and I had discussed Scharmal several times, and he thought she would be a good match for me. So, I drove many miles in 1970 to spend the Christmas holiday with Scharmal in her hometown, Kiowa, in south central Kansas. There her parents of Swiss-German descent owned and operated a large wheat farm.

Even with specific instructions I strained in the darkness to find the Schrock farmhouse. *All the farms look the same in the snow!* Exhausted, after 12 hours on the road, I shouted "Yes!", when I spotted Scharmal waving me in.

I'd been in touch with Scharmal by mail since our time together in Aspen. Along the way I'd shared with her my experiences at Western Illinois University, including news of fellow faculty member Gloria. Scharmal, Gloria and I had been students together in Cincinnati. The two women were both talented singers. They differed in physical appearance, but both had outgoing and sparkling personalities. Were they rivals? Yes, for the musical stage; and, I would like to think, for my attention.

On the first day in Kiowa, Scharmal and I visited her uncles and aunts in their farmhouses. In one house I overheard, "Aunt Susie is planning the wedding." *What!?* I had not at any time proposed marriage to Scharmal, nor had I even suggested the possibility, yet her kinfolk treated me as though I had.

Scharmal's mother charmed me with her gentle chatter; her father, less talkative, eyeballed me throughout my stay. Sheryl, the middle sibling, seemed more enthusiastic about my arrival than Scharmal. I imagined Scharmal had this thought in mind, *I'll wait and see what Edwin's intentions really are.*

Scharmal's brother Mark, the youngest sibling, proved to be the mischievous one. He wanted right away to take me rabbit-hunting with his dad. "There are so many rabbits here, and it's easy to spot them in the snow." *Why hunting?*

Mark, his father and I with rifles in hand ventured out in a pickup truck. Soon Mark spotted the prey. "Look, over there by the woodpile!" A few rifle shots later (I didn't fire a shot), Mark picked up the dead rabbits and proceeded to skin them in front of me. He kept staring at me. I guessed he expected me to be repulsed by the sight. I didn't blink, and he looked disappointed. Mark didn't know I had watched my grandmother killing rabbits and chickens behind our hotel, as well as prepping them for the frying pan. That's when I stood about three feet tall.

Indoor activities included the Ouija board, an entirely novel experience for me. Being a skeptic, I wasn't inclined to take the board's messages seriously, but in kindness to my hosts that evening I managed to fake some interest. The true enthusiasts, the believers, jumped every time the pointer moved to another letter in the alphabet. "What's it spelling?!"

"It's...uh...w—e... After a lot of stops and starts, the words emerged. A cousin announced, "Wedding bells!"

I glanced at Scharmal, who looked at me intently expecting some response. Instead, I stared at the Ouija board hoping to silence any more announcements.

I made no proposals, no commitments regarding marriage on that visit; nonetheless Scharmal and I and the rest of the family parted in good spirits. She and I hugged in the farmhouse doorway. She looked a little sad. I suggested she visit me in Macomb. She nodded slightly.

Near the edge of the village of Kiowa my car slid off the icy road into a ditch. I stood on the roadside hailing the very occasional passing car. Nearly an hour passed before a car stopped. I asked the driver to contact the local garage owner, who said he would bring his tow truck right away. While I waited for the truck, I reflected on my holiday in Kansas...

I'd considered partnering with Scharmal before my journey to Kiowa. I genuinely liked her; I enjoyed her company. The Schrock family had welcomed me, and so would all the heterosexuals on the planet. *This is a golden opportunity.* ***Don't waste it!***

Scharmal did visit me in Macomb in the new year. She stayed overnight with me, and we did have sex. I wasn't however making love to Scharmal; I'd only serviced her. She left Macomb probably as disappointed as I.

The day started as usual with Lisa dragging herself out of my bed. She wouldn't let me open the blinds or turn on the lights. I watched her trail off to the bathroom, while I shuffled along not far behind. She did her business and moved on to the kitchen and the coffee pot. I took a leak.

We were sipping coffee when I noticed the clock. "Hey, we have some extra time." Lisa saw my leering look and leaned over the table, her breasts falling out of her pajama top.

"You initiated this?" Dr. Campion asked.

"Yes. I reached over and gently squeezed Lisa's nipples. She tucked her hand in my shorts and fondled me. We groped awhile and kissed, and hurried to the couch."

"And then what happened?"

"Lisa pulled me on top of her. We fucked. I was exhaling, when I reminded Lisa her music analysis class was about to begin. She dressed quickly and left."

"Was it satisfying for you?

"Yes, and for Lisa too."

Dr. Campion was especially pleased when Lisa arrived on the scene in 1971, after counseling me for four years.

"Who is Lisa? Is she a student?"

"Lisa started her bachelor's degree at a college in her home state, Tennessee. She transferred to Western Illinois for her junior year, and she's studying piano with me."

"Tell me about her."

"Lisa's blond, blue-eyed, gregarious."

"Anything else?"

"She's pretty, and she's curious, and she has boundless energy."

At another session, about a month later, "How's it going with Lisa?" Campion asked.

"I gave her an engagement ring."

"What prompted this?"

"I look forward to seeing her every day. We're really comfortable together. I can imagine a future with her."

"Any doubts?"

"None. This is the right thing to do. I can feel it."

"Then go for it!" he said, with a big grin brightening his face.

When Lisa and I announced our engagement, my colleagues and friends congratulated me with gusto. Social approval greeted me at every turn. *Now I'm on the right path. No more guilt, no more shame.*

I took pride in escorting Lisa around town. She sparkled with her blonde hair and irrepressible personality. When we went into the jewelry store for an engagement ring, she declared for all to hear, "The bells will be ringing for us." We greeted everyone in the store that day.

In student recitals, Lisa played the piano very well, and she wore on stage the red velvet dress I'd given her. I sat there proudly beaming in the audience.

"You're no longer licking your lips, when you talk about men," my psychiatrist informed me.

———

Another month went by.

Sitting in my apartment I asked Lisa, "When should we walk down the aisle? Next summer?"

Lisa brushed back her blonde hair. "Next summer? Yes!"

Glowing, Lisa said, "Mom and Dad can call… no…I can call our Baptist Church for open dates."

Lisa moved into hyper drive. "I'll ask Susan to be the maid of honor…Uhhh … Sam, for the organist… and… Jane for…"

"Wait! Hang on! Before the planning begins, let's visit your parents. Let's all get acquainted. Hmm,…Christmas break is not far away. Let's drive to Chattanooga; afterwards, I'll drive on to my hometown."

"Christmas would be perfect! You could meet my parents and my grandmother. You'll love all the decorations at our house. Mom can never stop adding ornaments. Oh yes, (nodding her head) We'll be driving home in your **red** car."

I intoned in sing-song fashion, "People who drive red cars must be looking for a mate!" With a wink I said, "Is it time to let go of ol' Bessie?"

"You bet," she said. I matched her enthusiasm, even though something shadowed inside.

A few days later, Lisa and I were chatting about having a family. "I want at least two children, maybe more," she said.

"Don't chuck those pills just yet! We can talk about family, after you've finished your degree, and after we've decided what's next for your career and mine."

I can see there's no stopping her now. "Which church should it be? I mean, for their education?" Lisa pondered.

"Hold on! What's the rush? Do we have to decide now?" I asked.

"Of course, they should be raised in the Baptist church!"

I jerked backwards. "Are you sure about that?"

"Of course. You went to Sunday School, so did I, and they will too."

I gave up my Baptist membership in the '60s.

"Let me think about it." I said and walked into the bedroom, where I gasped convulsively. We'd never talked about educating our children. *Why is this so disturbing?* I couldn't let it go, our first conflict.

"Lisa, I need some time, some space."

She looked puzzled. "I don't understand. What's upset you?" She put her arm around my shoulder. "Tell me."

"How about tomorrow? Do you mind, going to your dorm?"

She sat back. "I want to talk about it now."

"Please…"

She shrugged and threw up her arms. She grabbed a few things from the bathroom. Then off we went to her dorm.

"My stomach is churning. You've got to tell me what's wrong…"

I didn't reply.

"Okay, okay. Call me first thing in the morning."

I ruminated all night about our future together. *Something's dead wrong. It's not about religion… What's been nagging me?* For several years I'd worked hard to be one of the guys, one of the straight guys; I'd dated and bedded a handful of women. And I had taken the very serious step of promising to marry Lisa. *Am I doing the right thing?*

Breaking the engagement will crush her, she wants so much to marry me. As for me, all my hopes on the straight path will be crushed as well. But…

It's time to confront the truth: *I can't honestly marry a girl.* It's time to shake the noose of conformity: *I can't live in someone else's shoes.*

By dawn, I'd decided to break the engagement.

Later that day, choking on almost every word, "Lisa, I can't go through with it. I'm so sorry. I just know it's not going to work out."

"I don't believe this. We promised each other…I **love** you!"

"I wish I could explain. I just know in my gut we have to give it up." *I'm too ashamed to tell her the truth.*

Lisa and I agreed we would talk again in a few days. I made it clear that I would not be altering my decision, yet she seemed to harbor some hope.

Days later, in my apartment, I spoke again to Lisa and apologized profusely. I urged her to complete her degree at Western or another school. With guilt aplenty I said, "The blame for the breakup? That's all mine."

To ease the separation I asked, "Would you still like a ride home for the holidays? I'll be driving to my home in a few days."

Lisa hesitated. "Yes," she said, wiping away her tears.

Soon we were on the road to Chattanooga. Conversation ran sparse, sometimes stilted, sometimes effortless. We limited ourselves to topics like our good times at Western and our families' traditions at Christmastime. We stopped for lunch in Paducah, Kentucky, where I pointed on the menu to, "Grits and biscuits. We're almost home!" Lisa smiled faintly.

Moving on towards Nashville, Lisa seemed sad, but not angry or vindictive. I felt miserable all ten hours on the road. *This trip is my penance for breaking the engagement.* As we approached Chattanooga, Lisa became tearful. I wanted so much to say the right thing, but I didn't know the right thing.

When we stepped out of the car at her home Lisa interrupted the silence, "I guess you'll need Bessie after all," as she gestured towards the car.

I didn't reply.

Briefly I chatted with Lisa's parents who looked at the floor more than at me. Both strained to hold to some semblance of civility.

"Mrs. Hudson, what a beautiful tree! The ornaments look like antiques. Are they family heirlooms?"

"Yes, many belonged to my mother, and to her mother," she replied looking at me for a moment, then back to the floor.

What can I say? At last, "My dad, he grew up in Chattanooga on Brainerd Road."

"We know that part of town quite well," Mrs. Hudson said.

No one spoke. The silence became unbearable. Staring at the door, I said, "I should be on the road again. It's late, and I have another 70 miles to go." It felt more like I had another 1,000 miles to go.

I took leave of her parents and exited with Lisa. On the porch I embraced her one last time and said, "Please forgive me."

She looked at me but did not respond, not a word, not even the blink of an eye.

I trudged to my car and waved. Sad, and relieved, I drove away.

"I can breathe. **I can breathe!**"

To be completely free I needed to tell my family and friends who I am. *Most of all I need to tell me!*

Back in Macomb, news of the break-up spread rapidly. Some colleagues treated me coolly, and a few townspeople stopped speaking to me. *Dr. Campion, what have I done? What have **you** done? Have you guided me wisely?*

I ended my therapy sessions on the phone, "No more appointments. I need a break, a **long** break."

Campion replied, "Are you sure you're ready to be on your own? Are you strong enough?" He started tapping into my perennial self-doubt.

"Ready or not, it's time for me to go it alone. Goodbye."

Four years had passed, and I had spent much of my small salary on conversion therapy.

Part Three

I didn't tell my mother or brother about my sexuality; instead, I indulged my post-engagement freedom in pursuit of men in gay bars, bathhouses and public restrooms. I may have thought, *I'm searching for Mr. Right*; I actually spent most of my time with Mr. One-Nighter or Mr. Fifteen-Minutes. Sexual addiction had quickly taken over my life, and it began to schedule my days.

In a rest area I met a broad-shouldered young man in a plaid shirt, jeans and work boots, and I invited him home. When we started undressing, I noticed he wore chicken-wire stockings and panties underneath the clothing I'd seen. In a blink, his manner changed to 'her' manner. *What do I do with this?* Not much. In a gay bar in Chicago guys in drag gravitated to me. *Why?* I still don't know. I do know I wanted a guy without a boa.

On weekends I sometimes trained to Chicago where I wandered the halls of Man's Country, a gay bathhouse, with a towel wrapped around my waist. One night I'd stopped in the doorways of a dozen private rooms and looked at guys looking me over. When no one showed any interest, I began to wonder, *Am I too skinny? Too tall? Not muscled enough? Is my dick not thick enough? Not long enough? Am I too old? Too young?* Each guy waved me on, no words spoken. Trial by a jury of one.

I usually scored several times; however, that night I wandered the bathhouse hoping for at least **one** welcoming word or gesture. When I thought the evening would end without any contact, a golden beauty waved me in. His blonde hair and his deep blue eyes were the first charms that grabbed my attention, then his trim, athletic body stunned me, and finally, there's more, he dropped his towel and turned towards the bed, showing me his blue-ribbon bubble-butt.

When I stepped into his room, golden boy looked at me with his long blonde lashes and said, "I love you." *I love you?* I had never heard those words in a bathhouse, aka meat rack. *'Desperation' must be writ bold across my face.*

As soon as we sat down on the bed, we started groping; then he rolled over onto his hands and knees, showing me his gorgeous butt again. Next, he pulled my dick to his aching hole. *O my god!* The ecstasy began when I plunged inside and his rim hugged me. *I'm in rectal heaven!*

Spent, we lay there wrapped around each other, his jism sprayed over the sheet. A perfect match, he's the bottom, I'm the top. And he's gentle and kind.

I knew of course this would be a one-time thing. The likelihood of seeing him again, nil. That's life in a bathhouse.

<hr>

During this period I reconnected with my colleague Burt who welcomed me back into his arms. In my absence he of course had not been idle. There had been multiple bed partners I learned.

"Let's have a threesome," Burt suggested one evening when Bill, a mutual friend, stopped by.

I hesitated. *Well, it's something new, but do I want to share Burt?* I did say yes.

I humped Bill and Burt humped me; our daisy-chain gyrated in rhythm. We were all smiling and singing, "<u>Hal</u>-lelujah!," <u>Hal</u>-lelujah!," when the cum came. Later, when we three were lying in bed, I looked at Bill and Burt sleeping, while I quietly whimpered. *Does Burt like Bill more than me?*

Burt was one sexy guy, tall, dark-haired, handsome and well-endowed. His touch electrified me. At the end of a work day, I often rushed to his house and threw myself into his arms. On more than one occasion though, Burt first walked me out into the yard, chatting, while some other guy, I figured out, exited through another door.

"Burt, these other guys…?"

"My love for you is **real**," he said.

I walked away shaking my head. *I need an **anchor**.* Where is my angel?

In the summer of '74 I flew to Austria to participate in the American Institute of Musical Studies. There I accompanied singers and coached German lieder with Harold Heiberg. We spent our first four weeks touring Vienna: backstage at the State Opera, a guided tour of Schönbrunn, and many other sites. At Demel's, I consumed more than my share of Zucher Torte and Kaffee mit Schlag. This Austrian sojourn allowed me respite from all the goings-on at home.

Four more weeks followed in Graz, Austria where Institute participants performed numerous concerts. After one of the performances I accompanied, Jan Meyerowitz told me, "You look like Gustav Mahler." I smiled. When he complimented my playing, I beamed.

Performing with Janice Perkins in Graz, Austria, 1974

I performed with a dozen talented singers, some were graduate students from top schools in the States, others were already pursuing music careers. Plus, I interacted with and learned from excellent voice teachers and coaches, such as Helen Hodam, Oberlin Conservatory and Marguerite Meyerowitz, Juilliard School.

We spent our last week in Austria at the Salzburg Music Festival where I heard, among others, Dietrich Fischer-

Dieskau singing Schubert's *Die Winterreise*. Dieskau captured fully the pathos of the rejected protagonist.

The festival's international audience responded in ways both surprising and amusing. When the staged performance of Berlioz' *Damnation of Faust* ended, the ladies, so patrician in their floor-length satin gowns, vigorously stomped their feet. Knees were **bobbing** that night!

We toured the Salzburg Cathedral where Mozart and Haydn had premiered some of their choral works. *This is the acoustic **they** heard!* That summer I reveled in Austrian heaven. I loved the countryside and the musical tradition. The summer mustn't end!

I returned to the States, floating just above ground.

Months before going to Austria I had decided to pursue a doctoral degree. I don't remember why I chose Boston University, but I do remember applying to BU and being accepted in the Doctor of Musical Arts program in piano. I began classes in the fall of '74 immediately after my wonderful summer in Vienna and Graz.

In Graz I'd met David, a pianist, who had recently graduated from Boston University. He shared with me his experiences at BU regarding the faculty, the facilities and the curricula, all of which prepared me for my next challenge. David also gave me a lead on housing that I secured near the university; it had been David's former residence, a rooming house. He fondly recalled the landlady, Miss Margaret, whose house sat on Babcock Street in Brookline. She was an elderly, heavyset woman with swollen legs and a big heart. She had never married, yet she nursed the man she loved at her home before he died. Miss Margaret told me she had brought him to her house directly from his hospital bed without a nod to the nurses. "He needed to be where he'd have the loving care he deserved."

From Miss Margaret's house I walked to the university for my piano lessons with Maria Clodes, a Brazilian by birth, who smoked cigarillos during our sessions. **That** took some getting used to. She was by nature nurturing, encouraging her students, enabling her charges. She also had a husband and three children at home, plus a few farm animals. She loved them all, just as she loved her students.

I had entered the doctor of musical arts program with trepidation, since I still lacked confidence as a solo pianist. *Maybe I can turn this around.*

I prospered with Maria, who wanted to be addressed by her first name. Maria introduced me to a relaxed wrist approach at the keyboard that has benefited me and my students ever since. She guided me, informed by her extensive solo and ensemble performance experience. She had been a child prodigy, playing her first solo recital at age six, featuring her own compositions, in the prestigious Teatro Municipal in Rio de Janeiro. Maria stands out as my best piano instructor. That year she introduced me to Schumann's *Phantasie*, Op. 17 and Beethoven's *Sonata*, Op. 109.

I also had a great rapport with my chamber music coach, Eugene Lehner, a violist in the Boston Symphony Orchestra. Lehner had been a member of the Kolisch Quartet that premiered two of Schoenberg's quartets. With me and two other grad students, Lehner shared his exceptional insights into Schubert's *Trio in B-Flat*. He also challenged us to seek alternative interpretations to various passages in the music. "Try it this way," he'd say, and he'd hum or play his viola, "now this way." That creative exploration has served me well.

I had taken off a semester from Western Illinois to begin the doctoral program, with a commitment to return to Boston in future summers to complete the required courses and recitals.

———

When I returned to Illinois, I met Oscar from Medellin, Colombia. He was a senior in the architecture program at the University of Illinois. Oscar had no car, so I drove from Macomb to the Champaign-Urbana campus to be with him. Our trysts in his dorm room were passionate. It wasn't long before he offered to move to Macomb and live with me.

"Are you giving up your goal... a graduate degree?" I asked.

"No, but I also want to be with you!" Oscar replied.

I'd met other young men who told me the same sort of thing. I suspect they all wanted someone who had a responsible job, someone who could provide a home for them. A few seemed desperate. One of them told his mother about me and my university position, because she'd said to him, "Queers can't get good jobs. They'll never amount to much."

Do I want someone to be dependent on me? It was challenging enough to take care of me. I only had a little money in the bank; and I tended to worry about the future. *There's no way I can help someone else.*

"My family kicked me out because I'm gay," Oscar explained. "Only my younger sister will talk to me." I did feel his pain; I didn't offer him though a key to my apartment.

Oscar had his attributes: charming, good-looking and smart. And, of course, that endearing accent. We continued to phone each other, and we met as often as we could.

The following year I visited Oscar in Philadelphia where he had started his master's degree program at Drexel U. With my sexual addiction in charge, I went to a gay bathhouse in Philly before I drove to Oscar's apartment. I felt a little guilty when he and I embraced that night. He seemed to sense what had happened. *Was it my body odor? My clothing? Why didn't he throw me out?* Because he liked me? **Loved** me?

The ultimate offense came in Boston when Oscar arrived for a visit. Right away I said, "Let's go to the bathhouse!" He expressed no interest, but agreed to go. We wandered separately through the corridors of anonymous sex with towels wrapped around our waists. When we crossed paths, I could see his distressed face, but he said nothing. He indulged me and my addiction. Finally, we left for my apartment, where we lay together. Oscar did not chide me for my blatant disregard; instead, he welcomed personal time with me. Looking back, *What a fool I was!*

Oscar and I agreed to meet one more time. The meeting passed pleasantly, but Oscar clearly did not want to let me go. "Are you **sure** this is our last time?" he asked. I nodded. He mounted me as he had before, yet much more intensely, because it would be the last embrace. Breathless and weepy-eyed he collapsed on top of me.

Later I reviewed our relationship and I sent Oscar a letter of apology. "Please forgive me for my callous behavior. You're a special person, and I abused you. Shame on me!" That was the gist of a long list of regrets. I don't recall a response from Oscar. I'd hoped he would be inclined to forgive me. I know my burden of guilt felt somewhat lighter when I mailed the letter.

A few years later I met Oscar again in Philadelphia where he had been designing houses and sharing his life with a new partner. His kindness, his friendliness, put me at ease.

What an idiot I was! Oscar loved me.

In my rented bungalow near Western Illinois University, I hosted a party for gay friends and acquaintances in the mid-70s. Some of my guests were students, some were faculty. At that time, I don't remember there being any gay social gatherings in Macomb. Somewhat anxious, I circulated the invitation.

I arranged with my friend Ann, an excellent cook, to cater the food for the evening. The guests appeared as requested in costume. Ann arrived in a maid's black uniform with short sleeves and a short skirt topped with a frilled white apron. A starched white tiara crowned her head and black lace stockings wrapped her legs. All the guys agreed, "She's hot!"

I greeted everyone in my Franz Liszt get-up. Sam, a hairdresser, loaned me a long, windblown wig for the piano wizard of nineteenth-century Europe. I rented a formal outfit with tails for the evening.

All the guests were chattering away when I raised my glass and said, "Welcome, one and all! Let's party!"

"Thank you for having us," I heard from several voices around the room.

There were no other places to gather in this small university town, except in private homes; gay bars were sixty-plus miles away.

After chowing down Ann's delicious meal, - a few were still licking the whipped cream on the strawberry pie off their lips - the guys started exploring inside and outside the house. Some were hanging out in the back yard, while others sat on the front stoop, looking across my narrow, grassed lawn to the wide, park-like median separating two residential streets.

A few had brought recordings and stayed indoors to play *Dancing Queen, I Will Survive, We are Family* and the list went on. The music didn't stop until…

Chris and Jim rushed in from the front porch yelling, "Somebody's throwing rocks at your house… at us!"

Oh, my god! What are we going to do? What am I going to do?

Soon all the guys came indoors and a few glanced out the windows. "What the hell?"

Some were cowering, like me. Others were figuring out what to do.

"We don't have to hide in here," Jack, a senior, spoke up. "Let's throw rocks right back at them."

Five rushed outside looking for rocks and soon began hurling them back across the grassy median. Two of the five, Charlie and Ebb, were lovesick freshmen from Chicago, who'd met at Western.

In the dim street light, the five squinted and were able to see several young guys hiding behind shrubs. "They look like college students," one of our boys said. "I think I recognize one of them," another added.

The wordless rock exchange went on for almost an hour. No one suffered an injury; and no rock had broken a window.

The perpetrators, it seemed, wanted to intimidate, rather than physically harm us. I remained inside for the duration. I admired, envied, the five who braved the rain of rock. When the culprits slipped away, the party came to a close with muted goodbyes. Relief finally came to me, when the street went silent and my bungalow receded into darkness.

One evening in Macomb I gently dropped sliced sirloin into a teriyaki marinade. My dinner guests, my land-lady and her sister and brother-in-law, glanced at their watches when I started stringing green beans.

I looked at my watch. *Damn! Dinner's already a half-hour late. When will I ever allow enough time for prep?* "Cover the beans with stock, shoyu, sugar and salt, and boil for 8 to 10 minutes uncovered to preserve the original fresh color of the vegetable."

The phone rang as I turned on the burner. My landlady picked up and called me to the phone.

"Edwin, this is Betty, Betty Burns (sister of my high school classmate Britt). I have some sad news about Britt." She started to cry.

"What happened? Is he alright?"

"He's dead!"

"Dead!? But...? How...?"

"He was murdered."

"What!?" I said shaking.

"He was found tied to his bed and... stabbed, over... and over again."

"NO! Sssssstabbed? Not Britt! I can't..."

"The police are investigating. So far, they have no clues."

"I can't believe!"

"I wanted you to know."

"Yes, but..." Still shaking, "Incredi...!" Gasping, "Is there, is there anything I can...?"

"No, my family has taken care of everything; but thanks for asking."

"How are **you**, Betty?"

"Oh, I'll be alright. I'm staying with my parents for a while."

"Such a shock! I'm trying to take this in."

"I know, it's hard."

"Please let me know, when you have news; and, thank you Betty...for calling."

"Goodbye."

"Bye."

I can't believe it! Ten years ago, Britt and I graduated from high school. *Now he's dead!?*

I turned to my guests, "Britt Burns, my high school classmate, is dead. His sister just told me he was murdered in his apartment, **murdered!?** Someone recently told me Britt's career has been going so well uh... (tapping forehead) in an engineering firm in Detroit."

"Do you want to have dinner another night?" Gayle asked.

"Oh no, please, I don't want to be alone right now."

I finished the cooking and we sat down at the dining table with wine glasses in hand.

The food had no taste for me. The conversation distracted me for a while. An hour or so later, dishes dried, my guests left. They knew nothing about Britt's sexuality, or mine.

Britt, murdered because he's gay? Did a 'trick' deceive him, kill him?

Betty said, "Britt was tied to his bed." *Was he into S&M? I'll probably never know the answer.* And I never did.

After completing a summer session at Boston University, I returned to Western Illinois University, where I greeted my old mindset. The discontent I had felt with my life and career over the past several years surfaced again. I had decided during those years there would be no more solo piano playing for me. Now, the department chair started pressuring me to play solo recitals. Feeling vulnerable I asked myself, *What should I do?* What are my alternatives? That's when the pendulum swung wide. *Should I be doing something other than music?*

At Western I accepted a part-time opportunity in the office of the Vice President for Development. In addition to my regular teaching load, I took on fundraising projects for the College of Fine Arts. After several accomplishments, the VP told me, "You've earned your salary for the year in less than nine months. Congratulations!"

That success buoyed my spirits and led to my next arts-admin adventure. A ballet company in Florida offered me the position of manager for a company seeking professional status. WIU granted me a leave of absence and I packed my bags. *I'm thrilled to be moving to another state and a new career.* I hadn't bothered to ask the fundamental question: *Am I prepared for this?*

Sitting at my manager's desk, the alarms went off when I realized: *I've never written a budget. How can I write the company's financial plan?* My attitude: I'll wing it! That proved to be woefully insufficient, and dismissal came six months later. "Head back to your **teaching** job," a board member told me, while he handed me a check for the remainder of my contract.

Back at Western Illinois I mumbled responses when my colleagues asked, "What happened?" One faculty member shared her hunch, "Someday we'll find out you were fired." *Bull's eye*, I thought, though I never admitted it.

Frustrated, I decided to leave my job at WIU and look for something else TBD. My colleagues questioned my decision, "Are you sure you want to give up your tenured position, and your associate professorship?" Others were incredulous, "Are you crazy?"

I thought a change of venue, a change of focus, would clear my muddled head; and I would be able to chart a new course. Just moving, moving on, may be enough.

I resigned my post at WIU; and I moved to Boston to complete the doctoral degree, taking with me a little courage, and a lot of uncertainty.

In 1982 mother phoned, "Cynthia, you know, Ed's daughter from his first marriage, she wants his address." What a surprise! Cynthia had never spoken with anyone in my family; and now, my half-sister wanted to contact her father, our father.

Mother made some calls, located dad in Mayfield, Kentucky and reported back to Cynthia and me. Cynthia's inquiry prompted me to contact him. I'd already planned to return to Macomb to pick up the remainder of my belongings. *Why not drive through Mayfield? I'll only add a couple of hours to my trip.*

With much anxiety I called my father, not knowing mother had already prepared him. "It's okay if you want to stop by," he replied. *The door is open!* I set out on my odyssey at 42. Twenty-five years had gone by since the divorce. *How will he greet me?*

Dad had sent me a brief note of congratulation and a few one-dollar bills for my high school graduation back in 1957, a few months after the divorce. In the mid-60s I'd sent my father a letter which I'd hoped would trigger a response. No reply.

In Macomb, Illinois, age 30, I wrote to dad again. This time he replied, "Let's write a song together. The crap I hear on the radio shouldn't be on the air. We'll show them how to do it! I'll write the words; you write the music." *He seems to be reaching out to me. Maybe we can do something together.*

Dad had been more or less pleasant throughout the letter. He closed with, "A musician is a man with a guitar stuck up his ass." I ripped that letter into many pieces and flushed them down the toilet.

"Why have you been wearing black?" a neighbor asked.

I'm in black? I was mourning the loss of my once-upon-a-time father.

During the early years of my parents' marriage, it's clear from the photographs that our family thrived together. Then for some unknown reason my father hit the road as a salesman for Olan Mills Studios out of Chattanooga. That's when our family unit began to fracture.

Forward to 1982, I now had an opportunity to reconnect with my father. *What will he say?*

When I arrived at dad's residence in Mayfield, Kentucky, I saw an old motel that had been recycled as a senior residence with minimal renovation. Even in the late afternoon light the exteriors obviously needed repair and fresh paint. His walls, all the walls, were tilting a bit westward.

Dad greeted me with a smile showing a total of four teeth in his mouth, and the four sat in the middle of his lower jaw. His flattened nose had been broken in high school football. Holding onto a cane he led me into his small, dimly lit two-room apartment, where I noticed the floor was covered in carpet samples of reds, greens, purples and yellows. The samples were not stitched together, and were free to travel about the room, no doubt assisted by the three resident cats. The cats had destroyed several upholstered chairs, leaving wads and strands of cotton padding scattered about the room. They had also pulled several of the venetian blinds to the floor, letting in the fading light and the neighbors' eyes.

While I was looking at the cats, dad remarked, "One of my cats is shedding and (pointing) his hair covers that end of the bed." *An apology?* No, an explanation.

I assumed dad had put on his best shirt, coat and trousers, even though they were frayed at the edges. He was now seventy-six. He had been – or still was? – a heavy drinker and smoker. His home looked shabby, yet he sat proudly erect in his cat-clawed chair.

We started chatting about my road trip from Boston. All the while we were carefully checking each other out. At first, I sat uncomfortably in my chair wondering if he might say something that would push me out the door. When I was a kid, he sometimes called me "Dingbat," a slur from a comic strip. I braced myself.

He surprised me with, "I moved to Mayfield, to these senior apartments because it's dirt cheap. I used to work this town, driving down from Paducah for a day."

"Are you still selling portraits?"

"I stopped years ago. No more quotas, no more deadlines. What about you? What are you doing in Boston?"

"I moved there last year to finish a doctoral degree. I recently gave up my job at Western Illinois University. Now I'm heading back there to pick up my gear and meet with a few friends." Words continued to flow from him and from me, motivated by the pressing question, *Who is this man who sired me?*

As a youngster and as an adult I had looked many times at photographs of my father from his childhood on, wanting to know more about him. I wanted to connect somehow. His Chattanooga High School photos held my attention every time I looked. In one picture he stood proudly in his football uniform; in another he smiled broadly in black-face for a minstrel show. *He must have been somebody… important!*

Now I looked at him up close, late in life. *Not so impressive.*

"Tell me about your family. When I was a boy, mother and I visited your stepmother in the hospital. She lay there dying of cancer. One of your aunts held me up, so your stepmother could kiss me on the cheek. Then your aunt hurried me out into the hall and rubbed my cheek hard with her handkerchief. "We don't want you to catch this horrible disease," she told me.

"Can't help much on your family tree," dad said. "All I know for sure… Boy, you is from de South."

That glib remark revealed dad's heritage had little or no value for him. While a boy he had moved out of his parents' home to live with his uncle, probably because he intensely disliked his stepmother. He apparently never looked back. In a subsequent letter, he did mention several family members who might be able to illuminate the family tree, with this caveat, "But they may not be alive."

A woman, short and pudgy, wrapped in a well-worn chenille bathrobe, stepped into the room. Startled, I jerked back, "Who's this?"

Dad introduced me to Ruby Grisham. "She was my crew chief in Olan Mills days." Without any greeting she said, "Ed really wanted to see Cynthia."

Not me?! I just drove over a thousand miles to be here.

I've never met my half-sister. If Cynthia's still alive, she would be in her late eighties. In my teenage years, I saw her photograph on the Society Page in *The Chattanooga Times*. Once she appeared on a horse in her riding togs, in an evening gown for her debutante party and in a cap and gown to receive her nursing degree. *How pretty she is.* I still have the photo dad kept of her as a young girl. Later in life Cynthia completed her MD training. As a full-fledged doctor, she'd called my mother for dad's address.

I turned towards dad, "You've collected a lot of recordings." He showed me some of the LPs piled around his chair: "Here's Bach... and Strauss... and Merle Haggard... and Louis Armstrong... and Glenn Miller, and a lot more (pointing at the stacks). I listen to the PBS station every week, to symphony and jazz, and Prairie Home Companion."

He astonished me with his keen interest in music. It's hard to believe this is the same man who warned me against being a musician years before. "Musicians are poor; be a basketball player!" I'd played basketball in high school, but I knew that was not my calling.

Dad didn't know some of the music terms used on the broadcasts from Murray State's PBS station. "What's a frog on a fiddle? What does "rondo" mean?" I answered these questions and others, and I promised to send him a music dictionary. He looked pleased.

"Do you miss traveling?"

"I used to," he said, "but not anymore. My body's slowin' me down. This week my doctor told me the same old story: SOB."

"SOB?"

"Shortness of breath. He prescribed another inhaler. It helps a little."

Sometimes the cats distracted us. Once in a while Ruby would add a comment. The topic of liquor prompted her to say, "Ed gave up drinking when my six-year-old granddaughter sat in his lap, and said, 'You **stink!**'"

Dad had tried to give up drinking many times. He'd participated in several rehab programs. The addiction however had held him firmly in its grasp.

Now a young girl, an innocent, had accomplished the impossible. *Is he imagining that his daughter Cynthia spoke to him?* Cynthia, whom he adored, was a young child when his first marriage ended.

Two hours had passed by. *This is the longest conversation ever with my father! He's spoken civilly to me; he's* **welcomed** *me.*

"Would you two like to go out for supper? **My** treat!"

"Yes!" they replied.

How often do they go out? They have no car and, looking around the room, very little money.

"Not many choices in Mayfield," Ruby pointed out. "Is KFC okay?" Off we went to Kentucky Fried Chicken.

"Everything tastes so good!" Ruby said, echoed by dad. On the way back to their apartment both thanked me several times.

In their doorway dad told me, "I called your mother and asked her to stop you from coming, but she had no way of reaching you. And now, after spending some time together, I'm glad...I'm glad you came. Come again, if you want." Even Ruby nodded her approval.

Are you two friends? Lovers? I hadn't heard any affectionate exchanges, no "dears," no "darlings." I hadn't noticed any touching either. Only a few words passed between them, probably only a few were needed, since they were longtime friends. It appeared the two had combined their meager resources; and they seemed to be content.

I left Mayfield elated. *I made **contact** with my father, maybe something will come of it!*

A few months later I received a call from Ruby Grisham, who said loudly, "Me and Ed, we're in the hospital and we're dyin'. What are you gonna **do** about it?" She had a gift for leaving me speechless. *Am I obliged to do anything for a sometime father and a woman I hardly know?*

"Ruby, I'll think about it. I'll get back to you."

I called a social worker in Boston who advised me to contact her counterpart in Mayfield.

"They're not dying," the social worker explained. "When they do, the state of Kentucky will bury them." It was no surprise to learn that dad and Ruby were totally dependent on welfare checks.

Then I gave the social worker some background information about dad and our family history.

"You don't need to feel responsible for them," she assured me.

I still felt the need to do something. I phoned dad, who expressed surprise that Ruby had called me. "We were back home from the hospital in three days," he said.

Almost a year after my visit, Ruby died in a nursing home of multiple problems, including kidney failure. Ruby's son arranged her burial without notifying Dad.

"He's heartbroken," his friend Gloria Burger told me. Gloria had met dad when the Olan Mills crews stayed in Paducah in her grandfather's hotel. Gloria's comment revealed Ruby's importance to dad. More than that, Ruby's dearness to him.

For the next four years in springtime, I made my way to Mayfield. Each time my father and I talked with greater ease. Between visits we exchanged letters and spoke over the phone. One of his letters began this way, "Dear Judejer (Junior), when you were very, very young, when anyone asked your name, you would say, 'Edwin H. Light Judejer.' You said many cute things when you were a child." Those words melted me.

In one of my letters, I obsessed about some problem which prompted dad's one-word response in large, hand-written script:

"R E L A X!"

I also sent him a recording of one of my doctoral recitals. "Enjoyed the tape very much," he wrote. "Gloria wants to borrow it so her family and friends can hear it." It pleased me that he liked the tape, and it pleased me, on one of our visits, when he introduced me to his friends with respect and admiration.

Dad and me, Colonial Hotel, Copperhill, TN, 1942

Before the third visit dad informed me that mother wanted to join us. "She can come, **if** she leaves her religion at home." When they were married, mother would beg, cajole and threaten him with God knows what, to attend church with her. He always responded with, "My soul doesn't need saving!"

Undaunted, mother persisted in her campaign to redeem him and resorted to any means at hand. She arranged for him to gift me a Bible; that is, she sent him a Bible, ready to be mailed. Dad included this note with the Book: "I'm sending you a Bible at your mother's request. She claimed I gave you one years ago, and you lost it, moving around so much. You can swap this Bible for the Koran, the Talmud, or a subscription to Penthouse."

"Your mother can come to Mayfield, **if** she leaves her religion at home." Had dad been staying away from mother and me in my childhood and adolescence, because of her religion? Did mother know what was happening? Her religious fervor may have deprived me of a father when I most needed him.

As a youngster I watched Dad leaving home to sell photographs for the Olan Mills Studios. He spent most of his time on the road, visiting us now and then. He saw me less and less.

Even though they had had no contact for twenty-seven years mother offered to spread her maternal wings over Mayfield. "I want to take care of Ed. I still love him."

Dad declined right away because, I assumed, he knew living alone would be far better than sharing a space with an overly solicitous housemate and former wife. Later though, he did defend her in a letter, "Your mother called on Easter Sunday. She is so proud of you. Please don't do anything to hurt her."

When I returned to Boston, I attended a concert of the San Francisco Gay Men's Chorus, the first gay chorus I'd ever heard, the first probably that anyone in the Opera House that night had heard. The exceptional quality of the concert and its positive message lifted my spirits and those of everyone in the audience. I ached when the chorus sang "We kiss in a shadow" from *The King and I*. When the song ended, I heard a collective sigh from the crowd. We (the many gays in the audience) all identified with the young couple whose forbidden love led to separation and punishment.

The Chorus sang full-out with pride. I left the hall thinking, *I should be, I can be, proud of me.*

At Boston University, I fulfilled the doctoral degree requirements over several years: two solo recitals and one chamber music recital, as well as classes, including music theory/analysis, music history, an elective in art history, plus language proficiency exams in French and German.

For the final degree requirement, I wrote a dissertation on the topic of Ravel's piano piece, *Jeux d'eau* (the fountain, the play of water). I spent more than a year writing and editing the paper, conferring with several faculty members who each had passages for me to rewrite. Professor Sheveloff, the principal reader, fine-tooth-combed every syllable of the document. "My professor made me suffer when I wrote my dissertation," he told me, "and, I'm going to make you suffer as well."

And suffer I did. The criticism never ended. When I thought a passage finished, Sheveloff told me, "Rewrite it again. Remove all the passive voice. Find a better example in the Ravel score to illustrate this point." And so it went, month after month. Discouraged, I trudged on.

Professor Sheveloff eventually signed off on my dissertation. A few weeks later I presented my thesis in a public lecture-recital. **It's over! I jumped all the hurdles. I'm Dr. Light!**

In the fall of '84, the new Fine Arts Dean Phyllis Curtin, the former opera singer, handed me my diploma. She smiled admiringly, when she handed me the Doctor of Musical Arts certificate on stage at the Boston University Theatre.

To celebrate, Mother and I toured by car the Maritime Provinces of Canada with stops in New Brunswick, where we watched in amazement the tides in the Bay of Fundy, and on Prince Edward Island, where we stuffed our bellies with lobsters and mussels.

In Boston I spent as much time in gay bathhouses as I had in Chicago. Loneliness and lust pushed me through the door and into a towel. For an hour or more, or less, I touched, I held, another man. Sometimes we exchanged names, sometimes the real ones. These strangers and I pretended for a short time to be longtime lovers, embracing each other with extraordinary passion. Then home again, alone. Sex substituted for love and compassion.

I needed to do something that would set me apart, something that would ring some bells. On the cruising grounds I began speaking with an English accent. *This is the ticket!* (BBC dramas on TV had left their mark.) I don't remember practicing the accent, maybe I should have. On the trail one night another cruiser looked me in the eye, and said with acid on his tongue, "What's with you and that phony Brit accent?!"

Damn! Just another face in the crowd.

"I'm caught on this mindless merry-go-round, and I'm not willing to let go," I mumbled.

One more trick, that's what I need. On the walls of public toilets frequented by gay patrons, I sometimes read this hand-written message: "Stop! This is de-humanizing!" Nothing could stop me.

The only check on my sexual activity, and only a partial one at that, were regular blood tests for the AIDS virus. Once I panicked because I'd had unprotected sex; but the test results were negative. Lucky me! Too, too many were not lucky.

With my sexual addiction in charge, I walked to Boston's popular cruising area, the Esplanade, seeking a bed partner for the night. Around 9:30 PM in August '85, with the Charles River flowing quietly alongside the park, I started touring the usual hot spots, the shrubs hiding couples in the shadows. I was there, we were all there even though, or maybe because of the risks, we were taking. Straight guys sometimes popped up armed with sticks and rocks and hammers; sometimes cops raided the bushes.

That night I walked as usual from thicket to thicket, looking for some action. When I turned another dark corner, a gang of five young men grabbed me. "We caught ourselves a faggot." They pushed me to the ground onto my knees. They slugged me, cursed me. "You're slime! We hope you rot in hell!" Four of them held me while the ring leader stepped forward and kicked me in the mouth with the heel of his black military boot. "You won't be sucking cock for a while!" he said and spat on me.

They released me and I fell flat on the grass shot through with pain. The gang strolled away, "Let's find another cock-sucker!" Ever so slowly I stood up, not fully conscious, and walked out of the park in my blood-soaked T-shirt. "Somebody please, somebody," I begged. "Please help me!"

A gay man came to my rescue, and minutes later I entered Mass General.

"You wandered from bed to bed totally crazed last night, screaming all the way," a patient told me the following day. Two days later an oral surgeon wired my broken jaw.

What I had dreaded for decades had happened. In my mind the attack was inevitable, because I believed faggots will be punished.

After nine days in the hospital, I returned to my apartment and my gay roommate who happened to be a nurse. Dan helped me deal with the physical pain: he monitored my meds; he prepared meals; and whatever else was needed. Lucky me, *Dan is here.*

With no prior knowledge of the bashing, mother called early on in my recovery. Dan picked up and described my condition. I groused; I didn't want her to know about the assault, certainly not its motivation. She knew nothing about my sexuality. The very next day she knocked on our apartment door. Boy, was I pissed. *She's going to make a lot of fuss and make me even more uncomfortable.*

The pain meds I took left me constipated. Dan gave me a laxative which did nothing to relieve the bowel backup. Mother heard me straining in the bathroom. "Let me in there, and I'll pull it out!"

Dan had a better idea: he tripled the laxative dose. Relief came none too soon.

I had two nurses for a week. That proved to be an asset, because I needed assistance, being unsteady on my feet and unsettled in my head. My wired jaw dictated a diet of liquids for two months. Mother and Dan did their best to vary my beverages, blending all sorts of nutrients with fresh fruit. At Mass General, my nurse gave me a menu that featured a hamburger with ketchup and mustard from a blender. *A blender?* I was puzzled and excited. *Hey, I can have a burger!* Then I drank it. *That's crap! That doesn't taste anything like a burger!*

When mother realized I was in good hands, Dan's and my doctor's, she returned to Copperhill and called me often.

Two months later the oral surgeon removed the wiring from my jaw. Despite repeated sedation I jerked with each pull on the wire, even with the surgeon's assistant holding my hand. Before the assault I wore two partial dentures from a high school basketball accident that left me with a broken jaw. Now I had more missing teeth, plus some jagged ones. *Please, nobody **look** at me!*

Before my teeth had been repaired or replaced, I started walking one day down West Newton Street toward Prudential Center. An attractive young man crossed the street to join me. His obvious interest brightened my mood. *He's checking me out head to toe.*

"Can you help me?" he asked. "I need to take the T (Boston's subway) over to Harvard Square. Which line should I take?"

While I gave the cutie directions, he noticed my mouth and the gaps where teeth used to be, plus all the jagged teeth. He stopped talking and walked away. My ego dipped to the ground and stayed there.

"Hope you are OK and your dental bill is not too burdensome," my dad wrote. "I haven't played the lottery until today. If I win, I will send you money for the dentist."

I consulted with dentists who estimated restoration would cost $7,000. *What?! I can't afford that!* Several months went by and people started asking, "Your teeth, when ...?" Steve, a friend, offered to speak with an attorney in his office about the state's Victim Assistance Program. Happily for me, the attorney intervened on my behalf and the state funded the dental expenses.

During the assault the bashers stole my wallet. The next day the gang used my credit card to buy jewelry totaling over $1,000. When they tried to use my card a second time, a security guard requested an ID and that led to the arrest of the ring leader.

Two policemen spread out a dozen mug shots in front of me. "Can you identify anyone?" I looked but I couldn't with certainty pick one. However, I did say while holding a picture, "If I saw this guy in the street, I would run the other way."

The cops told me they needed a positive ID in order to prosecute the person arrested. Because my mind had blocked the trauma, the policemen recommended I contact a hypnotherapist.

Before I made that call, I took a walk outside where I passed some construction workers in hardhats, and I almost said out loud, *Hey, do you want to beat up a fag?* My morale had sunk to an all-time low. The physical damage, though substantial, paled when compared with the psychological harm I'd suffered.

After a few inquiries I connected with a young hypnotherapist, who had just set up his practice. There couldn't have been a more sympathetic listener. Moving step by step, week after week, he prepared me for the ultimate challenge of revisiting the assault. He gained my trust with his empathy expressed in thoughtful queries, gently put. *He understands. He wants to help.* We proceeded on this quest hand in hand.

In one of our sessions, I told the hypnotherapist about my earlier experience with a psychiatrist, the one who tried to convert me into heterosexuality. The therapist responded quickly, "He should never have done that!"

Weeks later the hypnotherapist carefully set the scene: "Imagine yourself in a theatre where you are viewing a play. You can bring down the curtain whenever you want." He guided me into a kind of trance, a wonderfully peaceful state. I confronted the assault without reliving the shock or the pain.

Three months into hypnotherapy I reviewed the mug shots. I singled out one photograph. "This is the picture you pulled out on the first round," the same two cops told me. The first time I saw the photo, trauma had blocked my recall of the assault; the attacker's image though had escaped the shield.

With an ID in hand a District Attorney prepared to prosecute. In the first court hearing I saw the gang leader with one of his pals. They smirked at me. The leader, whose name I've long forgotten, stared at me with heartless eyes. I went rigid and gazed at the floor.

"When and where did this happen?" the judge asked.

"Eighth of August. After a movie I walked to the Esplanade, about nine o'clock."

"What was the movie?"

"Survivors." The court clerk chuckled, glanced at the judge and quickly returned to recording the hearing.

My case slogged through the courts for more than two years. Because a huge backlog of cases preceded mine, several assistant district attorneys advised me. One of them told me, when I testified in a probable cause hearing, "Carefully consider your answers." After several procedural questions, a jurist asked me to describe the assailant. I paused. *Try to remember the face, the photograph. Try to **calm** down.* Finally, I said, "He has a square, flat face." That seemed to satisfy the jury. There were no more questions.

A trial date had been set; I appeared but the defendant did not. This happened three times. Frustrated and angry, I asked an assistant DA, "Why isn't he here? Why can't the cops pick him up?"

"There are so many cases. That's probably not going to happen."

In 1985-86 the local and national media were focused on hate crimes. In Boston, two TV stations interviewed me. I remember one exchange in which I related all the details matter-of-factly. "But how do you **feel** about what happened?" the reporter leaned in to ask. He looked me over and turned to the cameraman, "Shut it down." That's after I began crying.

I became a minor celebrity. People who saw me in my workplace or in the street praised my courage in speaking out. I even addressed cadets at the police academy. Several of them asked about my health afterwards. *They're really concerned.*

Months later an assistant DA informed me the defendant had been shot in the forehead gangland style. "The case is officially closed," I heard from the DA's Office. A friend winked and asked, "Did you arrange the hit?" I shook my head.

Hypnotherapy helped me to deal with the mental agony. Ever so slowly I distanced myself from that August night. The shock and pain of it tempered my behavior for the next several years. I steered clear of places in Boston where harm might come my way, particularly gay cruising areas at night; and I usually walked after dark in the company of friends. The fear abated over time, but not completely.

Can I ever accept myself?

Part Four

After the assault I didn't report to work at the Huntington Theatre Company for almost two months. During my recovery I began the taxing repair and replacement of my teeth with removable partial dentures. Thanks go to the grad students and faculty at the Harvard Dental School.

I started working at the Huntington while completing the doctoral degree. I served as HTC's house manager and company manager, the first running the front-of-house operation, ushers and concessions, the second managing the actors' housing and general welfare. Not distinguished administrative posts to be sure, but they paid the rent and then some.

When I interviewed for HTC, the Marketing Director looked at my resume and said, "You're overqualified for the job!" I shrugged and said, "I'm looking for work."

A year after Dean Curtin had handed me my D.M.A. diploma in the Boston University Theatre, she saw me in the same theatre greeting the audiences for the Huntington Theatre productions. I worked at HTC for six years. Each time she entered the theatre she said, "It's always good to see you." Her face however questioned me, "**Why** are you still here?"

"Are you still here?" I heard from one of my ushers I had not seen for a couple of years.

Okay, why am I still here? Before the Huntington Theatre, I had managed the office of the. Arlington Street Church in Boston and raised money for the Powers and All Newton Community Music Schools in Boston suburbs, and played the organ and directed the choir in the Unitarian-Universalist Church in Norwell on the south shore of Boston.

The HTC jobs brought some satisfaction, but not quite enough. *I'm stuck; and I really need to get me out of this cul-de-sac.*

———

In the Fall of '85, back on the job at the Huntington, I proceeded with another project, the rehearsals of my one-act musical play, *Billy's Buddy,* that I had written in the spring of that year. Dental work had started, but my mouth still did not look normal. Fortunately, my participation on stage required no singing or speaking.

I walked on silently as Billy's buddy/the daddy of his dreams.

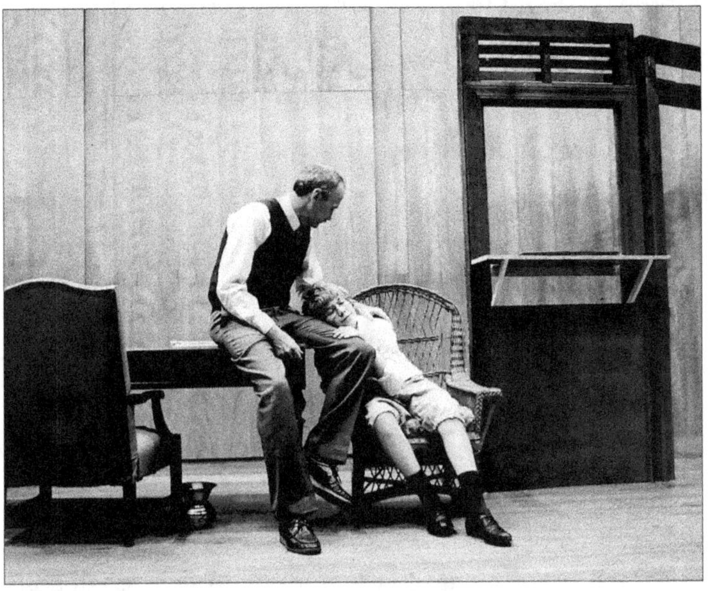

The Dream Sequence, *Billy's Buddy*, 1985

I had to contend with thoughts of the August assault throughout the casting and rehearsals of this play about my childhood. The play focused on Billy's desire to bond with his absentee dad at Christmastime in the late 1940s. Even though childhood memories of heartbreak and longing re-surfaced during the rehearsals, the production of the play provided a much-needed diversion while I recuperated from the assault.

Before the play's opening my dad wrote, "Had friends over from Paducah. They wanted to know the plot. All I could tell them, 'It would cost $5 to find out.' As they say in show-biz, 'Break a leg!'"

In review, the play is at best a sketch, but it does communicate Billy's emotional state through my lyrics and Richard Cornell's evocative music. One of the attendees greeted me with tears after one of the performances and asked, "Will there be an Act II?"

I staged *Billy's Buddy* at the Longy School of Music in Cambridge MA in November 1985. The wail of a train passing in the night had been taped by one of my colleagues at the Huntington Theatre. Other Huntington staffers transformed the *Look Homeward, Angel* set, just used at HTC, to fit on Longy's small concert stage. I'm forever grateful to the HTC team who supported my production and me in my recovery.

The presence of the set for Ketti Fring's play, about Thomas Wolfe's early years in a boarding house, inspired me in my modest effort that is rooted in the same Southern tradition.

I shared with my dad the tape recording and script of *Billy's Buddy*. He responded with:

"Bravo! I enjoyed it! – put me right back in Copperhill and the Colonial Hotel. I did all the chores you did."

"You cleaned the spittoons?"

"I did! Now keep up the good work. You're not too far from Broadway."

Dad never spoke about his presence in the play. Maybe he would have been uncomfortable talking about it, or, more likely, he saw no need for it, since we had reconnected.

During my recovery, my reawakening, I ventured out of academia for a solo performance. In downtown Boston in the French Library, I played a piano recital for a capacity audience. A friend had publicized the event and my recent adversity in the local gay newspaper. I ended the program with Gershwin's solo version of the *Rhapsody in Blue*. A piano professor at the New England Conservatory complimented my performance.

Not every minute of the visits with my father in Mayfield, Kentucky, pleased me. More than once his hatred of black people surfaced, leaving me quite upset.

On one visit dad shared this story about his upbringing, "My uncle thought niggers were a blight on the earth, and he taught me to throw rocks at any coloreds walking in our neighborhood. I'd hide out in the bushes and toss the **biggest** rocks I could find."

"Dad, I don't share your bigotry. You have to park your hatred while I'm here. Are you willing to do that?"

After a long pause, he nodded.

A bias that upset me even more was his contempt for gay people, like his rant on the male lead in *Saturday Night Fever.*

"John Travolta! John **Re-volta**! That fuckin' fag should be kicked in the balls, if he has any, and tossed out of show biz," Dad said.

"He can dance, he can act, he can…," I replied.

"Queers don't deserve to be on the big screen."

"As far as I know, Travolta's **not** gay."

"Oh, he's gay alright. Just look at the way he moves!"

Not brave enough to tell my father face-to-face, I wrote him a letter announcing, "I'm gay." I'd listened to him put down gays several times in his apartment. He believed, "AIDS is the Gay Plague." Dreading his response, I delayed opening his letter.

"I wanted to have some grandchildren," dad wrote. "But since you're in a creative field, it's okay that you're gay."

I heard no more attacks on queers. *I can't believe it; he's accepted me as I am!*

When dad needed to buy food or see his doctor, he ordered a taxi. Wherever he went he steadied himself with a cane. Even if he only walked a few yards, he would complain of shortness of breath, a telltale sign of a lifetime smoker. His alcohol addiction had led to the removal of part of his stomach, forcing him to eat several small meals every day. He could only chew soft food, and that slowly, with his four remaining teeth and his gums. His body was collapsing, just like the walls around him.

Despite his circumstances dad rallied when I arrived in Mayfield. Our visits buoyed his spirits and mine. No more "maybe tomorrows." We were connected.

Once he surprised me with, "I gave the cleaning lady five bucks to touch her tits." I grinned, while he relished the memory. *He still has fire in that potbelly.*

On my fourth visit he announced, "I won the lottery! I won fifteen hundred smackeroos! I bought some new clothes, a blazer and a pair of pants. I took a donation to the PBS station, and I bought a CD player, a really good one!"

His excitement overflowed, "I want to create a school for artistically talented young people."

I sighed.

In October of 1987, the fifth year of our bonding, my father died; a seizure had taken his life. When I heard the news, I felt my heart breaking. *He's gone!* **No** more visits, **no** more dad.

Red, the manager of dad's senior residence, found him slumped in his tattered chair, two days after his death according to the coroner. Red contacted me straight away.

"When I die," dad had said earlier that year, "just throw me in the ditch," pointing outside his window. I chose cremation.

"Just throw me in the ditch?" Why did he place so little value on his life? He was intelligent and curious about the world. He wrote just months before he died, "In Alcoholics Anonymous I learned that yesterday is beyond recall, tomorrow is but a dream, live for today. I still dream. Dreams and curiosity keep me going. I want to know what is going to happen and I have a dream or two I want to come true before I pass on." I assumed the school for the artistically talented was one of them. That letter ended with, "Love, Your always hopeful dad."

Dad had graduated from Chattanooga High School with honors and attended the University of Chattanooga for two years. He appeared to be on an upward trajectory, he seemed to be ambitious; but something interrupted. His addiction to alcohol took hold at age 16. I will never know why, because he rarely shared any of his personal history.

In Copperhill mother and I climbed to the top of Cemetery Hill, looked down at the former site of the Colonial Hotel and cast dad's ashes into the wind. Tears trickled down as we watched his remains drift in all directions on that windy day. We nodded to each other; yes, we'd made the right choice for the traveling salesman.

Mother broke the silence, "This is the closest we've been emotionally in years!"

"You're right," I replied.

We smiled at each other with dad's dust in our hair.

Cynthia, dad's daughter, whose inquiry had inspired the search for our father five years earlier, never called or wrote to him. Her loss, in my view. Dad had welcomed me back each year, allowing us to forge a bond of friendship, kinship. Knowing that he cared made me a happier and more confident person.

A few weeks later, back in Boston, a letter arrived from Dad's friend Gloria. "Ed may not have expressed it directly, but he really loved you."

He really loved me! I've waited so long to hear those words. I cried and cried.

Part Five

On my birthday in 1990 at age 50, I resolved to give up casual sex. I'd joined Sexaholics Anonymous with weekly meetings that revolved around testimonials from gay and straight men and women. I couldn't believe how many **gay** men and women attended those gatherings. It became clear to me the gay community needed a wake-up call.

I spoke a few times at the S.A. meetings. Once I began with "Lust has me on a leash..." We all shared how many months had passed in sobriety. S.A. rewarded us with a plastic coin for 4 four months, six months and so on. Everyone applauded each other's accomplishments. I didn't think I could do it, but I did!

I'd made a commitment to seek a meaningful relationship. Along the way I'd told my family about my sexuality. My mother reluctantly stopped introducing me to potential wives in my hometown. In time she told me, "When you meet someone (a man), who truly cares for you, I will be happy."

I had lived in fear for nearly forty years, afraid to be me, afraid to be queer. I wonder now why it had taken so long for me to accept who I am. Did I not believe my friends and family truly embraced me? Did I have such a low opinion of myself that I couldn't imagine any positive assessment? The latter hits the mark. Besides living in fear, I had been punishing myself for being gay.

Circumstances did change. On my birthday in 1991 - I'd been 'sober' for a year - I met Jack, a hefty guy with brown eyes and hair who bubbled over with energy. I doubt I would have picked him out of a crowd before the dinner party, but I learned that night there's more to discover.

Jack and I had been invited separately by mutual friends in the South End of Boston for my birthday dinner. Our hosts, Steve and Will, wanted to invite a fourth person to the table who had an interest in music. Jack sang at the time in the Brookline Chorus. That evening he amused us with stories of married men, the 'hetero' variety, who invited him to the Park Plaza Hotel for 'good times.'

Jack and I had briefly met a year before in the same condo for a large gay gathering. I remembered he had surrounded himself with a group, talking nonstop, pontificating to be precise. He obviously enjoyed being the center of attention. A year later that impression gave way to a more favorable one: It's not always about **him**.

After my birthday dinner I offered a ride to Jack, who usually rode the subway home. He accepted my offer that saved him considerable time on the subway, plus a bus ride to his house in Arlington, a western suburb of Boston. I lived in the next suburb only a few minutes away.

"That was a fun evening. Would you like to get together again?" I asked.

"Sure, but I'll be away on business for two weeks. You could give me a call then."

"Okay, I will." Jack tells me now that he wasn't expecting a call.

On the day he returned I did call. "Edwin who?" he asked.

Hmm. I explained...

"Oh yes, now I remember."

I suggested we share the cooking of a recent menu in the *Boston Globe*. He agreed, and we set a date.

Looking back Jack recalls, "This guy is charming and clever; he wants to check out my cooking skills and my house." At the time I just wanted to know him more than superficially.

The evening passed pleasantly for both of us. We enjoyed the meal, and conversation flowed. Next, we moved to the living room and starting talking on the couch. That's when Jack began groping me, and I pulled away.

"Why not?" he asked.

"I want to know you better." I had decided in advance, *No sex tonight. We first have to get acquainted.*

Pissed, Jack stood up and walked to another chair.

I'd not had sex for more than a year, because I had vowed to keep anonymous sex out of my life. However, holding to that commitment challenged me more than I expected. The stress constricted my throat when I said, "I just can't. Not now!"

The night ended awkwardly. *Will we ever get together again? Should we?* Jack may have been thinking along those lines too, when the conversation jarred to a halt.

"Goodnight. We can talk later on," I said.

Jack nodded, sort of.

On the way to my car, *Now, what do we do? What do I do?*

In the weeks ahead we did share a few meals, and we talked on the phone.

One evening in front of Jack's fireplace with logs burning bright, I decided, *It's time.* Clothes came off and we started exploring. Not many words passed between us. I did look into Jack's brown eyes and say, "You're handsome." His eyes beamed.

From then on, we were together almost every night after work, either in his house or in my apartment nearby. On weekends we went on day trips to many places in New England, often to Ipswich, Massachusetts, where we browsed antique shops and galleries. Jack collected Depression glass at the time. In Ipswich, we always took time out for fried clams and shrimp netted that day.

On one of those outings, I learned Jack had been in therapy for the previous four years. "My goal was to be comfortable as a gay man, especially so in corporate America." He went on, "I grew up in a small town, Emporium, Pennsylvania. That's where Sylvania manufactured radio tubes. Being gay there wasn't easy in the 60s."

In the 70s when Jack returned home on breaks from Syracuse University, his mother quizzed him about coeds. "Have you met any interesting girls?"

"No, Mom!"

"And why not?"

Walking away Jack said, over his shoulder, "Mom, that's none of your business!"

Minutes later Jack overheard a conversation between his mother and father.

"Did you hear how he spoke to me?!"

"Thelma, don't you know? … Jack's not the marrying kind."

For three summers 1989-91 in Thun, Switzerland, Scharmal, my longtime friend, hired me to accompany Swiss singers in a workshop of American songs. Scharmal's sister Sheryl, who lives in Switzerland, had made most of the arrangements. Sheryl is also a musician, a flautist.

What an opportunity this was for me, making music or hiking in the Alps almost daily! I can't imagine a more exhilarating way of living. Scharmal knew hiking would be too strenuous for her, so she stayed behind, while Sheryl and I explored hiking trails throughout the Bernese Oberland, including Kandersteg, Kleine Scheidegg and Lauterbrunnen.

Climbing upwards in the Alps taxed me enough, but coming down mountain paths proved to be even more of an issue for a novice like me. I didn't know how much pressure I'd be putting on my toes as we descended.

"Sheryl, look at my big toes; the nails are black!" The nails in time fell away. No such problem the second summer when I wore sturdier hiking boots.

Scharmal and me, Thun, Switzerland, 1989

Each summer I performed with Swiss singers and with Scharmal, an excellent soprano. Some of the Swiss singers were advanced, singing repertoire like Barber's *Hermit Songs.* Besides introducing these singers to American song, both popular and classical, Scharmal also helped each singer with any vocal issues he or she had. Scharmal's technical instruction truly impressed me when two college students, who had limited vocal talent, produced pleasant sounds. Brava!

In the workshop sessions I marveled at how easily I could play Steinway pianos built in Hamburg, Germany. It seemed effortless to play rapidly-moving passages. *The piano is playing itself!*

The Schrock sisters and I traveled in and around Thun when we were free. Sheryl easily maneuvered her small-scale Mercedes through the narrow streets and around the ever-present switchbacks. One weekend we went to Leukerbad for its healing waters. We splashed and reclined in one pool after another. Scharmal pointed, "Over there, let's try the Stone Grotto." After a few hours we walked to our hotel nearby where the sisters invited me to their room.

As we were laughing about something, Scharmal asked, "Do you remember how we used to mess around?" *What?* The sisters leaned forward to hear my response.

They're expecting me to jump in bed with them?! What do I do? This is so damned awkward!

"I haven't slept with a woman for at least fifteen years," I said. That announcement came out of nowhere.

Both women looked surprised, especially Scharmal. I was more than a little surprised myself.

"I'm seeing a guy named Jack." *I've finally admitted to the Schrock sisters who I am.*

"Is he **fat**?" Scharmal asked.

Scharmal was a large woman. She assumed (I guessed), since I had shown an interest in her in years past, that I would seek the company of overweight men.

"Jack's stocky," I replied.

Scharmal huffed.

The conversation halted. The evening came to a close without the usual laughter. Silently I walked away.

The personal rift however did not compromise our professional obligation to the vocal workshop. All three of us were smiling and chatting the following Monday when classes resumed. Both sisters remained cordial to me for the rest of the two-week session.

A year later I introduced Scharmal to Jack in Santa Fe, where the three of us shared a rented condo. We had all flown in to see several opera productions. We shared meals out, we cooked meals in. Jack, inspired by the occasion and no doubt by the desire to impress Scharmal, created his most elaborate breakfast menus to date, starting with fresh-cut fruit drizzled with Triple Sec, elaborate omelets with sour cream, etc. And afterwards, we toured northern New Mexico by car. Scharmal and Jack, both gregarious, became friends early on. When Jack left us for a moment, Scharmal turned to me and said, "You married well."

The three of us would gather again in the years ahead.

In 1992, more than a year after we first met, Jack and I decided we should try living together. My rent contract would expire in August near Jack's birthday, the 25th; and that's the day we scheduled my move-in.

Over the past year I had met several of Jack's friends from his Syracuse University days. Secretly I spoke with them about a surprise birthday party for Jack. Everyone agreed, "Let's do it! We'll all bring food and wine."

As Jack and I were unloading my belongings, he spotted first Andy, then Lin and Gary, and Peggy and… "You invited all my friends?!" Jack, surprised and pleased by the turn out, looked at me with a big, approving smile.

"This is the most stability I've had in my life in years!" I told Jack early on. His silence suggested, "Let's wait and see." I knew without a doubt, my life is starting over again with Jack, my angel.

When I moved in, Jack had been working at Liberty Mutual for 15 years, paying a mortgage and planning to renovate his home. The house still had its wallpaper and paint from decades ago. Together we took on the renewal of the house, at the same time our relationship began to deepen. We were making all decisions together, the challenging ones and the easy ones.

"What do you think, Jack, will plum wallpaper be too dark in the living room?"

"No, plum will make it richer; and look (holding a sample), how it ties in with the colors in the new sofa."

I nodded my approval.

"What about the mantle, and the moldings?" I asked.

We flipped through several color cards.

"Let's not go with pure white, it's too stark."

"How about this one?"

"It's too…gray."

"This is the one…it's cream-colored, just a hint of yellow."

"That's it! That'll work."

We hired a painter and a paper-hanger. "The room looks absolutely stunning. Eat your hearts out *House Beautiful, Architectural Digest*, et al!"

———

Two of Jack's Syracuse University classmates, Gary and Linda, married; and when their son Stefan was born, they asked Jack to be his godfather. Jack and Stefan bonded before I came into the picture. When I did, I joined Jack at various events in Stefan's youth including a high school musical.

That night when we walked down the hallway to the auditorium, I noticed a message on computer paper, the kind with punched holes on the borders. The message, writ large and taped across the top of a bank of wall lockers, read: "ATTITUDE IS EVERYTHING!"

I didn't pay much attention at the time. Later, that message gained currency for me.

In 1992 cousin Kay called to say, "Aunt Tootsie (my mother) is stumbling down the street. She's drunk! You've got to do something." My brother, who lived closer to our hometown, drove to Copperhill.

When asked about the imbibing of liquor, mother said, as she had often said before, "I have a little vodka at bedtime to help me sleep." We figured she must be 'going to bed' throughout the day, since her short-term memory had started to evaporate. Mother had also spoken about feeling lonely. "Most of my friends have died," she said with a sigh. The bottle had become her friend.

My brother phoned, "It's time. Mother needs our help. She needs to leave Copperhill." We discussed options in Boston where I lived and in Savannah, his home. We decided Mother would prefer warmer winters. Byron promised to check out senior residences in Savannah. After a careful search he and his wife Jan secured an assisted-living residence, Savannah Commons.

When it came time for mother to leave the town and the people she had known for most of her 83 years, sadness overcame her. A farewell party at First Baptist did ease her departure; all her well-wishers that day hugged her with tears in their eyes.

Along the way to Savannah and in that city in the months ahead, mother would often say, "Let's stop at the liquor store." Up to this point we were not fully aware of her addiction. When I visited her in Byron's house, I observed her raiding his liquor cabinet several times a day.

"Mother, you just had some gin."

"No, you're wrong. I haven't had any today." Later...

"Mother, you're drunk!"

"I am **not**!"

Byron's solution worked well: Cold turkey! He emptied his liquor cabinet, stashing its contents out of sight. Months went by, then no more, "Where's the bottle?"

Two years passed more-or-less peacefully at Savannah Commons. One night in '94, her trumpet case in hand, mother pushed aside the security guard at the main entrance of the Commons and walked across the lawn to a row of private homes. She knocked on door after door asking for help, "I want to go home. I want to go to Copperhill."

The Commons manager summoned Byron. He escorted mother with a policeman's assistance to a local

hospital, where a physician diagnosed mother's condition as Alzheimer's disease. "Your mother should be in
a nursing home." *Yes, but where?*

Several days and nights passed in Byron's home
where mother was up and about at all hours, urinat-
ing everywhere she went, causing nonstop havoc. Relief
came a week later when a room opened at a nearby nursing home. We were lucky; some families had been waiting much longer for a space.

In the nursing home over the next two years
mother gradually lost recognition of her family and
friends. Mother did recognize my brother Byron, because he visited almost every day. When I took her out
to lunch with Jack, on our visits to Savannah, she always
thanked, "Two lovely strangers for their kindness."

What surprised me, in the last years of her life, was
mother's ability to play the piano as she always had. In
her infancy two of her siblings were scuffling over a box
of matches while holding her. Distracted, they dropped
her, crippling her left hand and arm for life. Using the
side of her left hand, mother struck single bass notes,
and with her right hand she played the popular tunes
of her youth, *Bye, Bye Blackbird, Mighty Lak' A Rose*
and *Brother, Can You Spare A Dime?* In the chorus of
the last one, mother sang along addressing her nurs-
ing-home neighbors with feigned heartache, *"**Brother!**

*...can you... spare... a **dime?**"* A few of the residents smiled, some stared at the floor, while one clapped quietly. These tunes had pushed through her memory loss; for a few minutes, mother, the woman we knew and loved, reappeared.

In early February, 1998 the phone rang, "Come soon!" Byron said. "Mother's stopped eating. She's lost a lot of weight. Come now!"

I flew to Savannah and hurried to the nursing home where my mother's gaunt body shocked me. "Get her up; she needs to walk," Byron told me. "Get her to drink some Ensure." I managed to lift her up and onto the floor. We walked the full length of the hallway. On the return she wanted to stop in the TV room where several patients sat motionless, mouths hanging open, with glazed eyes fixed on the screen.

Mother and I conversed a bit. Words didn't flow from her lips anymore; they came in spasms. My name came up. She paused and slowly sorted things out in her mind and said, "I have a son named Edwin."

"I'm your son." Mother leaned forward and kissed me on the cheek. With a faint smile she slipped back into her silent world. She died two months later near her 90th birthday.

Byron carried mother's ashes back home to Copperhill. For the graveside service I inquired about a trumpet player in my hometown. The high school principal recommended a music teacher on staff. I sent her copies of mother's favorite popular songs, such as *Toot, Toot, Tootsie, Goodbye.*

At the gravesite a few relatives and friends gathered and heard mother's beloved minister, Grover Jones, speak glowingly about Frankie Mae. I also spoke. I spoke from prepared remarks with the support of Jack, who held me up on one side, and the minister on the other.

It wasn't easy saying goodbye. In the eulogy I mentioned conflicts with my mother, religion being one, my sexuality another. "She did come round to accept me and my choices, more or less."

During the service I looked at my brother Byron. He said nothing, his face blank, his eyes dry. *What is he thinking, what is he feeling?* He had looked after mother's needs month after month in the nursing home, always reprimanding the staff if they ever neglected their duties. Later I told Jack, "Byron must be exhausted. He didn't say a word at the service. Probably all accounts are settled, and he's at peace."

Mother, my stalwart single parent, supported me in good and bad times. She loved me, and I loved her, even though we didn't always express it.

Mother and me, before her illness

The trumpet sounded often in the memorial service. The opening notes of *When the saints go marching in* were the first to break the cemetery's silence. More tunes followed, like *Bye, Bye Blackbird*. After the service I offered a check to the trumpeter. "I can't accept it," she said. "I'm beholden to your mother. It was Miz Light who played duets with me in high school. She's the one who encouraged me to be a musician."

At mother's wake the night before, I greeted high school classmates and townspeople who had known and admired my mother. Jack stood beside me. The urn holding mother's ashes and the open case displaying her King trumpet sat on a table nearby. Mother had had a lifetime of music-making in Copperhill and the surrounding region, known as the Copper Basin, as well as in Chattanooga where she played in an all-girl orchestra in the 1930s.

Four decades had passed since my high school graduation and I needed to be reminded of who's who in the reception line. My longtime friend Mary Louise whispered the names of classmates and townspeople as they approached me. I listened to glowing remarks about Frankie, how she had helped them in so many ways. I learned that night about mother's matchmaking skill with a couple at First Baptist. "She brought Steve and me together. At our wedding, Frankie stood with us, as our Maid of Honor (at 80). We'll always remember her!"

Also in the line was Big D, the stud I'd admired in high school. He and his wife shared their memories of mother. Weeks later, after Jack and I had returned to Boston, I picked up the phone and heard the voice of Big D's son for the first time:

"I want you to know how much my partner and I appreciate your exchange with my dad. He's never really accepted his gay son; and he's never welcomed my partner. You opened his mind. He was so impressed by you and your partner; he described you as responsible adults. Thank you! Thank you!"

For five years I'd tried to convince Jack that having a dog would be a good thing. He reluctantly agreed, with this caveat, "We have to walk them regularly or we'll be shampooing the new carpet … a lot!" I knew I would probably do most of the dog-walking. Even though I had a full week teaching piano and playing the organ and conducting the choir for church services, I would still have more time at home than Jack, who tended to work six-day, even seven-day weeks.

First, we considered greyhound rescue dogs. We visited several rescue kennels, but Jack thought greyhounds would be too large for our house.

Outside one of the greyhound kennels, we were walking a potential adoptee, when Jack spotted another breed. "What's this?"

"That's a whippet," the owner told us.

"**That's** the right size for us!" Jack concluded.

I frowned. I really wanted a greyhound. My short list did include whippets and greyhounds, dogs with even temperaments and easy-care coats. "Okay, a whippet it will be!"

After some research we located a whippet breeder in the middle of Massachusetts. Shirley Cooney thoroughly questioned us to be sure we would be fit parents for one of her dogs. "Why don't you take Eleanor Rigby and her brother Billy home for the weekend," she suggested. "And we'll talk on Monday." We agreed, novices that we were. The two dogs were nine months old and neither had been in a car. On the ride home, which lasted over an hour, Ellie threw up repeatedly on the back seat. No problem for Billy. He rode like a pro.

Chaos ruled that weekend. Our first time out and we were baptized in flames. Billy often tried to mount his sister, who didn't seem to mind; she frequently licked his dick. Both were chewing anything plastic. And, we were reminded, they had never been in a house. Built to run, these two sight hounds raced through every room knocking over whatever stood in their way. Shirley, knowing we were inexperienced dog owners, should have sent us home with one dog, not two. Monday morning didn't come soon enough. On the way back to the breeder we agreed to keep one dog, Ellie.

A year later Jack reviewed the situation. "You know, Ellie's all alone much of the day; she **needs** a companion. Let's go back for a second dog." This is the guy who originally wouldn't consider having one dog in our home. Soon Chai joined our family.

Jack with Chai and Eleanor Rigby, Cliff Walk, Newport, R.I., 1998

Our two whippets, Ellie and Chai, spent most of their indoor time in our new family room rolling about on the carpet and sleeping on the new gold-colored couch. One Sunday after Jack and I had left for a church service, the two dogs feasted on a whole cooked ham they'd pulled off the kitchen counter. We thought we'd pushed the ham out of reach. Ha! We'd underestimated the dogs' determination and ingenuity. Only the ham bone remained, licked clean.

And where were the angels when we walked in? Two sick puppies were sitting on the gold couch surrounded by bits of ham splattered over the new cushions.

In May 2004 Massachusetts became the first state in the nation to legalize gay marriage. Jack and I were early supporters of the campaign for marriage equality. We urged our Unitarian-Universalist congregation to contact our legislators. We contacted our friends in Massachusetts by phone and email asking them to lend their support. Jack became a volunteer for Massachusetts Equality and knocked on the doors of state lawmakers.

We were among the pioneers who formalized our relationships in matrimony. At the Unitarian-Universalist Area Church in Sherborn, MA, where I served as organist-choirmaster, we proclaimed our vows on July 17 in front of 100+ friends and parishioners.

In six weeks Jack and I had planned the wedding. We consulted the minister, a photographer, a cake specialist, the church's hospitality committee and a 'flower lady' in the congregation. Jack followed through with all the details.

I invited a jazz trio, friends of mine, to perform for the ceremony. The musicians so impressed the audience that applause followed every tune. For the recessional the trio played Jack's pop-song favorite, *Teach Me Tonight.*

The most memorable reading in the service: this quote from Anne Morrow Lindbergh's *Gift from the Sea:* "When you love someone, you do not love them all the time, in exactly the same way…We insist on permanency, on duration, on continuity; when the only continuity possible, in life as in love, is in growth, in fluidity…"

At the reception a Klezmer violinist, a colleague of mine, strolled through inspiring all of us to lift our glasses. Several of our neighbors greeted us. Folks from out of town hugged us. Our friend Ortelio flew in from Chicago. Family traveled from Houston and Savannah and Atlanta. Jack's mom Thelma embraced us. My hetero brother Byron, who had escorted me down the aisle, told me at the reception, "If this makes you happy, it makes me happy." I learned afterward Byron wasn't sure he could participate in a gay wedding. Jack's brother Jason walked him down the aisle without hesitation.

Jack and I were charged with making a toast. Jack, who has never been at a loss for words, raised his glass first and started speaking. After several remarks he begin to dwell on the difference in our ages (Jack's 12 years younger). I became annoyed and raised my glass, "Here's to younger men!" The single gays and the single women, and a few of the married ones, lifted their glasses with me and cheered loudly, "To younger men."

Jack and me on our wedding day, July 17, 2004

The new minister, Nathan Detering, who had thoughtfully prepared the ceremony with us, welcomed all who came to the first gay wedding in the parish. The church women had polished a beautiful silver service for our reception in the hall the church had rented next door. It warmed our hearts to witness the joy, the love expressed in word and deed by the congregation and by our friends and family who attended. Such a happy day!

Days later Jack handed me a newspaper. "Have a look."

"What's this? Boston Globe...Food..."

With a big grin, "Do you recognize it?"

"No way! This is the menu for our first date... when we shared the cooking. You **saved** it?!" Jack has saved many things, rose petals from his mother's memorial service, his grandmother's Christmas ornaments, my valentines and this menu from 1991, the year we met.

I smiled and shook my head, "You sentimental sweetheart!" And I squeezed my squeeze.

In 2007 Jack retired after 33 years of service at Liberty Mutual. In the reception line at the corporate head-quarters, I stood beside Jack as we greeted more than a hundred of his colleagues. All of whom spoke warmly of Jack's tenure, praising his accomplishments. Everyone treated us with kindness and respect. An affirmation we treasure.

I had retired from piano teaching at the Indian Hill Music Center in Littleton MA two years earlier. IHMC faculty and staff hugged me on my departure. "You're leaving behind a trail of excellence," one of my piano colleagues told me. The same colleague performed in a program I'd just produced for the New England Piano Teachers Association that explored Bach's *Anna Magdalena Notebook.* "We will remember this program for a very long time!" a teacher told me.

At the same event another teacher handed me a recital program of my students at the Cincinnati College-Conservatory of Music dating back to the 1960s. "I enjoyed my piano lessons with you at C-CM, and I thought you would like to see this program." *Unbelievable!* "I'm stunned and delighted. Thank you!"

At Fitchburg State University, located west of Boston, I taught a humanities course that embraced music, art and literature appreciation. The Humanities Department Chair, Dr. Jane Fiske, also a pianist, wrote in her evaluation, "Dr. Light is an excellent teacher, pianist and colleague who has been a wonderful addition to our department."

The same year we had to say goodbye to our affectionate whippet Chai, whose liver had failed to function. We'd watched her become disoriented: she turned in circles repeatedly. It pained us, but we had to let her go. Chai had been family for eleven years.

Jack and I now live in New Mexico, more-or-less retired. I'm still performing, and Jack has been advising a nonprofit. After a few years in our new home, Eleanor Rigby, our other whippet, joined Chai in dog heaven. In 2017 we drove to East Douglas, MA to pick up our second pair of whippets. In route we stopped in Cincinnati to visit my alma mater. While we were walking on UC's campus, I tripped on a buckled sidewalk and dislocated three fingers on my left hand. An ambulance rushed me to UC's hospital, where two female surgeons reset my fingers and told me to commence physical therapy no later than two weeks. We cut short our itinerary, picked up the pups and headed back to Albuquerque for PT. Two and a half months later I resumed playing the piano.

Exactly one year after my fall I performed solo in a Santa Fe concert series for an audience that lifted my spirits with accolades. I'm not a great pianist; I am however pretty damn good. Am I note-perfect? No, but nearly so. That evening the music of Bach and Poulenc came alive.

In the past I only dealt in absolutes. If there were any flaws, I threw myself into the pit of self-loathing. Today I respond more often than not to fumbles with forgiveness. I remind myself: Don't lament the past, learn from it and dwell in the present.

What a joy it is to be me, now that I'm comfortable in my own skin! Mind and spirit free. Zen Buddhism has helped me achieve balance and peace in my life. Challenges of course still come my way; and when that happens, I meditate.

Jack and I recently celebrated our 31st Anniversary. Over those thirty-one years we've disagreed, quarreled, pouted and whined; and most of the time we've settled our disagreements by the end of the day. We've traveled to Europe, Southeast Asia, Central America and across North America; and wherever we go, we walk together with pride.

Acknowledgements

A special thanks to my principal editor, **Robert Spiegel**, who pushed me and encouraged me to express myself in more convincing language. "Make it live!" And to my beta reader, **Sarah Baker**, who, with her seemingly endless supply of energy and enthusiasm, guided me to do my best.

Thanks to my enabler in the self-publishing of my second book, **IngramSpark,** that led me through all the steps needed in the printing and marketing of the written word. I am also grateful to **Darlene and Dan Swanson** of Van-Garde Imagery for their creative skills and cooperative spirit in the design of this book.

Thanks to the **Word Sherpas**, a writing group in our neighborhood, that critiqued several chapters, leading of course to a better book.

And, thanks to my partner of 31 years, **Jack**, who helped me when my knowledge of the world of computers waned. He rescued me so many times. Otherwise, there would have been no book to read.